Embroidered Church Kneelers

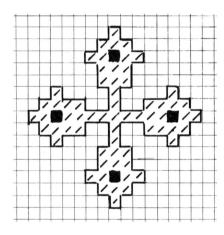

Contents

Acknowledgements

We are most grateful to the following for their assistance: Mr and Mrs Edwin Taylor, of South Pasadena; Mrs Alice Robertson, of Hamilton, Ontario; The Deans and Chapters of Winchester, Lincoln, and Chelmsford; the incumbents of so many churches who have been extremely kind and helpful in answering our questions and letting us take photographs; Sylvia Green for photograph 84; Beryl Dean for photographs 21 and 22; Trevor Williams for photographs 74a and 74b; Audrey Mitchell for printing the photographs; Mrs Maire Barton and Mr and Mrs Widdess for their help in showing us so much of Guy Barton's work, and for the loan of publications about it; the many, many people from all over the world who took the trouble to write to us with details of their kneeler schemes; all our friends and relations who took us to see churches in remote places; J. C. Trewin for invaluable encouragement and advice; Margaret Rivers, of the Embroiderers' Guild, and the subscribers to *Church Needlework News*, for helpful information; and, at all times, Miss Rachel Wright, of Messrs Batsford, for her generosity, patience, and expertise.

B.T.
W.T.

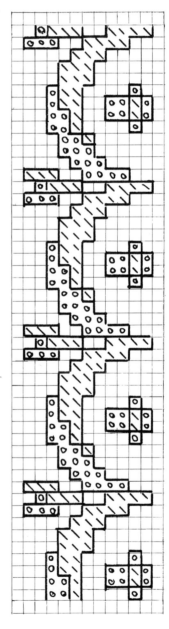

Note

In *Antique Needlework* (Blandford Press, 1982) Lanto Synge says:

The words needlework and embroidery are nearly synonymous. The former is general, embracing in its widest sense ordinary work such as knitting, darning and seam making but it also includes embroidery, which more specifically suggests decoration or ornament. In old records, 'embroidery' normally refers to work in silks. But ... 'needlework' often refers generally to decorative stitchery. The term 'needle-point' is applied in America to canvas work.

In this book, when we refer to schemes in America, we use the term 'needlepoint'.

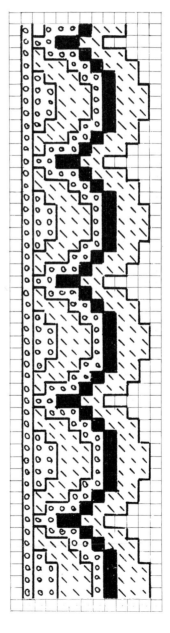

Introduction

Our beginnings

Wendy Trewin writes: When I asked an American friend what she had enjoyed most during a tour of the West Country, she replied promptly: 'Kneelers'. That, so far as I am concerned, is how this book began. Until then my only experience of kneelers had been of those in Hampstead Parish Church, designed and organized by Barbara Thomson; and of seeing the embroidered birds and flowers on entering the west door of Exeter Cathedral. They could hardly have failed to excite me because I am a Devonian and have loved our wild flowers ever since a botanizing aunt showed me the difference between the male and female primrose.

Most moving of all the sets of kneelers I have known since that day in Exeter are those that furnish another cathedral – Winchester. Moving because here embroidered kneeler projects began. Having seen what Louisa Pesel had done for the Bishop's private chapel, Dean Selwyn suggested that she should provide the stalls and seats in the choir with kneelers and cushions. She agreed. 'Only a woman of rare courage and imagination would have undertaken such a task,' he said. In 1938 she was appointed Mistress

1 Kneeler designed from the ancient floor tiles in Winchester Cathedral, in use in the Lady Chapel. Designed by Louisa Pesel, using tent, long leg, rice and gobelin stitch.

of Embroideries at Winchester. (See also page 12.)

During the Second World War she taught the girls of a school evacuated there to make kneelers for the Lady Chapel, and because she believed needlework to be therapeutic as well as decorative, she sent wool and patterns to prisoners-of-war in Germany. A rare spirit indeed.

*

Barbara Thomson writes: I suppose the real beginnings of this book are away back in 1961 when we discussed making canvas work kneelers for Hampstead Parish Church as part of our first stewardship campaign. At that time, though little information was available, the Embroiderers' Guild was very helpful, and I found its booklet *Canvas Work* for churches most useful. I

went to see the kneelers in Winchester Cathedral, dated 1932 and still looking marvellous; so, encouraged by this, and armed with Beryl Dean's *Ecclesiastical Embroidery*, with its excellent instructions on 'making-up', we started the project.

A small committee was formed, including, besides the two of us who had suggested that the kneelers were in a desperate condition and should be replaced, the church architect (whose mother was an embroiderer, so he understood what we were talking about), a designer, and an artist.

I went then to visit some cousins in Central Africa. While I was there, a tree-rat ate a hole in the middle of the sample kneeler I was working – and I learnt the hard way how to cope with holes in canvas.

Because most people were apprehensive of anything complicated we decided to keep the designs as simple as possible. The church of St John at Hampstead has very positive architec-

2 Kneeler designed by Barbara Thomson for the parish church of St John at Hampstead in 1962. Two shades of blue, and gold, using cross and rice stitch.

ture, and we wanted to enhance it rather than to compete. Bearing in mind the stained glass windows behind the altar, we selected (in the church) the appropriate colours from Appleton's crewel wool range. At first we used three different background colours, but when the first ones were completed, we eliminated some of the colourways; these are now to be found in the side aisles or the balcony. Three different background colours are too many, and I would advise against this. We ended up with two, blues and reds, and they are placed in the pews so that the same design and background are together. But kneelers seem to have a life of their own, and I am convinced that, as in the best fairy stories, they have a party in the middle of the night and get caught in the wrong place at dawn. How otherwise do they get in such a muddle by midday on Sunday, when they have been put right on Saturday? To overcome this, one background colour, or two tones of the same colour, will make for a much less chaotic effect.

3 St George's, Thriplow: the Smithy, worked in cross stitch.

I have now visited a large number of churches, and without doubt the most impressive schemes are those with carefully considered colours. It is astonishing how much variety can be achieved with a limited palette on a standard background.

Many churches have started with kits from one of several firms who offer them. For the inexperienced this can be an excellent way to start; but it has been lovely to hear from those who had done so, and who then felt brave enough to try their hand at designing their own – with splendid results and tremendous satisfaction. An example of this is St George's, Thriplow, Cambridgeshire, where the kneelers show aspects of village life, and there are also some that have been designed specially for two elderly gentlemen to make. Between them they made 20, and they are superbly worked and most effective.

Some churches have not controlled in any way either the colours used, or the designs; in practice the effect is not always happy, though sometimes this can have great charm.

The true beginnings

This book has been an adventure. You arrive at a church; it may be locked; you find a note on the door: 'Key at—'; or no note at all. You look for the vicarage (you become an expert at recognizing them from afar). The church may be a beautiful medieval building, or of airy Georgian proportions; it may be damp and crumbling, or lovingly cared for and smelling of polish.

Unless the kneelers are so craftily placed that they are the first things to take the eye as you enter, you will peer hopefully into the pews. If you have known nothing in advance, you may be in for a surprise. Thus, at one village church with unusual painted-wood panelling that cries out to be embodied in the kneeler designs, you discover disappointing coarse canvas, harsh colours and lumpy fillings in kneelers made unimaginatively from kits. At your next call, in a building of no great distinction, the kneelers are among the best you have ever seen. Their colours complement those of the floor coverings and the stained glass; the subjects reflect local topography; and thought has gone into the whole operation, down to the arrangement of kneelers in the pews – and, importantly, a filling which is both kind to the knees and will last.

*

To a newcomer the greatest surprise seems to be the age of kneelers (or lack of age). 'Aren't there any old ones?' is the question. 'Not really,' you say, and it is then that eyes glaze over with withdrawn interest. We are not sure why kneelers are expected to be old; perhaps because church furnishings generally are, or perhaps because when well designed to go with their surroundings, kneelers do give the impression of 'belonging'.

In any church they are often the newest adornments. Few are more than 50 years old; many have been made during the last two decades. The first documented project began in Winchester as recently as 1929. This was inspired by the indomitable Louisa Frances Pesel, a Yorkshire woman born in Bradford in 1870, who settled in Hampshire in 1925. When her old friend Bishop Woods, formerly Vicar of Bradford, moved into Wolvesey Palace, she offered to provide cushions and kneelers for his private chapel, then unfurnished. So it was that, under her supervision, Wolvesey Canvas Embroidery Guild was born. Its work is still in the chapel, adding immeasurably to a plain interior.

Louisa Pesel's choice of colours – soft blues, greens, mauves, and yellows – is restful and satisfying; her designs are impressions of flowers, leaves, crosses, and stars, without being overtly pictorial. The kneelers fit under the chairs, have rounded corners, and are thinner than the usual kneeler today. Naomi Royde-Smith called them 'praying mats', and one understands why.

When Dean Selwyn saw Miss Pesel's work, he wondered whether she could widen her scope. The great Cathedral had no such embroidery as hers. That was enough for Miss Pesel; in 1931 the Winchester Cathedral Broderers was formed under her direction, with her friend, Sybil Blunt, as designer. The word 'broderer' had some significance for Miss Pesel; in 1914 the Worshipful Company of Broderers presented her with a gold chatelaine as 'an award of honour in recognition of all her work for the study and revival of embroidery in England'. Her activities had not been confined to England; she had spent five years in Athens as Designer to the Royal Hellenic Schools of Needlework and Laces, and in the vacations she travelled further and studied wherever she went. On her return to England the Victoria & Albert Museum commissioned her to work a set of samplers. She became President of the Embroiderers' Guild in 1920.

Financed by the Friends of the Cathedral, the Winchester Broderers met twice a week in a room in the Close. For the designs Miss Blunt used her knowledge of heraldry and local history, while Miss Pesel tried out various ways of turning them into embroidery, constantly unpicking and trying again. When at last she was satisfied she would look at her experiment in the place for which it was planned. Her perfectionism was boundless. She gave instructions about the wool-dyeing which had to match exactly her specifications; her colour sense was unerring. Whatever the other colours, she insisted on the use of three shades of blue, something that gave unity to the contrasting designs. After much thought it was decided to work on coarse linen hessian; petit point centre pieces, worked by the more expert Broderers, were spliced into surrounds which could be done by the less experienced.

Finally, the Broderers completed 360 kneelers, and many other items: alms bags, cushions, a lectern carpet, furnishings for the bishop's throne, and so on, and these were formally presented in 1936.

*

4 One of the original kneelers designed by Louisa Pesel for Winchester Cathedral.

Louisa Pesel, although over 70, continued teaching during the war. When Atherley School, Southampton, was evacuated to the Deanery, she gave the girls the task of making 55 kneelers for the Lady Chapel, with designs inspired by the medieval ceramic tiles in the Retro-Choir. She told the girls that this would be their thanks-offering to Winchester for housing them safely. Without doubt, they learnt from her a great deal more than embroidery.

How she obtained materials during the war is a mystery. When local knitters became desperate, she placed in all the libraries boxes where oddments of unused wool could be left. With characteristic economy she evolved a way of making hospital shoes for local patients from remnants and pattern books of stair carpets. She died in 1947, and, at her funeral, the pall she made for the Cathedral – considered to be her finest work – was used for the first time. Dean Selwyn said of her: 'She gave her time, her money, her artistic talent, her sense of colour, her power of teaching and organizing, all to beautify the Cathedral she loved.'

*

Nearer our day, another great designer, Guy Barton, created the ten altar kneelers on a theme that concentrated upon gifts to the Cathedral, from a tenth-century manuscript (the Benedictional of St Ethelwold) to the modern lighting of the choir and choir stalls, a gift of the Friends.

5 Detail of two doves pecking at grapes, from the Tournai marble font, probably installed in Winchester Cathedral in the twelfth century during the bishopric of Henry of Blois. This is one of the medallions on the altar rail kneelers designed by Guy Barton for Winchester Cathedral.

6 William of Wykeham, from an altar rail kneeler designed by Guy Barton for Winchester Cathedral.

7 Winchester Cathedral: detail of the altar rail kneeler showing the transition of the window arches. Designed by Guy Barton.

8 Winchester Cathedral: detail of the altar rail kneeler designed by Guy Barton from the thirteenth-century tiles of the Retro-Choir.

The two central kneelers contain portraits of Bishop William Wykeham and his master mason, William Wynford, whose 'gifts' to the Cathedral were in its transition from Romanesque to Gothic. In the background of these kneelers the round Norman arches on one side give place to pointed Gothic on the other.

The Friends commissioned the altar kneelers to commemorate their Jubilee. Techniques and stitchery follow the Pesel tradition, and colours match the blue upholstery of the choir seats, the gold of modern oak fittings and the greys of the floor and stonework. Before the set was complete Guy Barton died of lung cancer in 1981. Unlike Louisa Pesel, his ecclesiastical work was not confined to Winchester. For 20 years he was art master at Marlborough College, and when asked to design stall cushions and kneelers for the school chapel his first action was to study Miss Pesel's embroideries and Lady Hylton's at Wells. Next, he started on seat cushions and hangings for the previously open-backed choir stalls in Lancaster Priory. This was a major undertaking in which his wife, Maire, herself an expert needlewoman, helped enormously by teaching the inexperienced members of the embroidery team.

All over Lancashire, in town and country churches, you find examples of his work:

St Paul, Brookhouse
St Paul, Caton
St Bartholomew, Colne
Coppull Old Church
St Michael, Croston
All Saints, Habergham
St Peter, Heysham
St Michael, Kirkham
Lancaster Priory
St Andrew, Leyland
St Paul, Little Marsden
Holy Trinity, Morecambe
St Paul, Scotforth
St James, Shirehead
St John the Baptist, Tunstall

The formidable list also includes one in North Yorkshire: St Alkelda, Giggleswick

Sir Norman Warwick, an Old Marlburian, made two of the stall cushions for the College chapel. For more than 30 years he held important posts for the Duchy of Lancaster, which maintains the Queen's Chapel of the Savoy. When he suggested that Guy Barton should design embroideries for this small building just off the Strand, Guy agreed, and repeated some of his Lancaster Priory designs. But apart from Marlborough and Winchester and these in London, we think of him generally in terms of the northern churches. This was inevitable. A Northcountryman by birth, he and his wife spent holidays and their retirement in their beloved Pennines. (See also *Crosses*.)

9 A simple interweaving design in rice and gobelin stitches, at St Paul's, Caton, near Lancaster.

10 The kiwi of New Zealand, from Christ Church, Woking.

PART ONE

Practical Considerations

Preparation

Before you can embark on a kneeler scheme, you need to spend some time in preparation. As in any work of art, this can be dull, but it is essential to the final result. Consider the following questions:

How is the work to be paid for?
Does the vicar/rector/incumbent want the scheme?
Does the church council/vestry approve?
Will it contribute? In kind? In cash? Or in labour?
Do you have an experienced embroiderer who can help the amateurs and beginners?
Are the kneelers to be made up professionally? Or do you have an upholsterer in the parish who can do it for you? Or do you have to learn how to do it yourself?

Design

Before you begin to think about the actual designs, ask yourself where the kneelers will be when not in use. On the floor? Or hanging from the pew/chair in front? By one hook, vertically, as at St Clement Danes; or by two hooks, horizontally, as at Christ Church, Woking; or propped against the back of the seat as at St Mary's Cathedral, Edinburgh; or on a shelf below the seat, as in the OBE Chapel of St Paul's Cathedral?

These considerations may also affect your design.

1 How deep do the kneelers need to be? This, do not forget, depends upon the height of the seat from the floor, as well as the distance from one pew to the next. The easiest way to answer is by trying different depths of kneeler in the church, and also by asking a variety of people to try them out. Remember that it is easier to

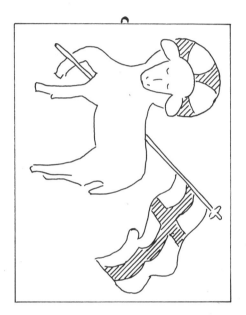

11 Sketch showing how a design which looks odd when hung sideways, can show well when hung horizontally.

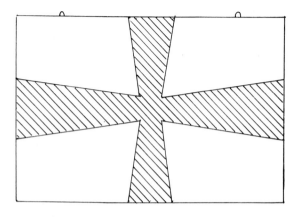

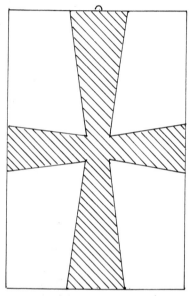

12 Sketch showing a design which works well whichever way it is hung.

get down on to a kneeler than to get up, especially if you are not in your first youth. Even half an inch may make all the difference. I found the London telephone directories very useful here: you can add or subtract different thicknesses easily, until you arrive at the optimum.

2 If the kneelers are to be very deep, then it may be that the sides should be upholstered and not embroidered. Again, if they are very deep, it means that they will probably be too heavy and clumsy to hang up satisfactorily.

3 If they are to be on the floor, you may want to give them a solid base with small feet, and possibly a 'lug' to hold, so that you can adjust them easily to suit yourself.

Scattered through this book, you will find some charted motifs and borders. These are intended to be of help, so feel free to copy them, adapt them, or let them be the starting point for your own inspiration. There are no completed charts because we hope that the book will encourage you to make your own.

Hazards

Guy Barton, who designed such lovely canvas work for many churches, disapproved of embroidered kneelers in a pew because people would use them as footstools. Whatever one does to deter them, people will put their feet on kneelers. One has to accept this and allow for it when designing. When colouring a carpet design, colours are chosen not only to accord with, but also to 'read' against each other, and often the paler colours may be slightly brighter or stronger than expected. This is to allow for a degree of soiling when the carpet is used. Wool has the marvellous quality of wearing clean, and though your kneelers will get a little soiled in time, they can be vacuumed and shampooed just like a carpet.

Bearing this in mind, design your kneelers so that it will not upset you to see other people's feet on them in the pews, and keep fine work for areas such as the altar rail (where they will only be knelt on), or for that used by servers and acolytes.

Another hazard is that liquid brass-cleaning fluid, if it spills, does something horrible to wool, and you will find bleached patches on your work. There is no way to correct this except to unpick the affected parts and re-embroider. So if your altar rail is of brass, do arrange for kneelers to be removed or covered when the rail is cleaned, as accidents will happen.

Colour sense

Design is probably the most important part of a kneeler, but choice of colour comes a close second. Colours can be too bright or too pale, or

13 & 14 Differences that can be achieved by working the same design using different stitches. Found at St Mary the Virgin, Great Shelford. 13 (*above*) is worked with a blue cross stitch background, with the fish in several tones of grey, using tent, upright cross, and long leg stitch. 14 employs tent stitch for both the background and the fish, but with the stitches on the fish lying in opposite directions.

unsuited to the surroundings, or just plain dull. There can be too many of them, or too few. On the whole one background colour is enough; two at most. If they are bright and the designs are strong, the effect as you enter the church is restless. We noticed that red, blue and green backgrounds were one too many at a church which (since the kneelers were beautifully designed, worked in a variety of stitches and professionally finished) shall be nameless. A pity.

On the other hand, reds and golds make a sudden flash of colour in the rather dark church of St Mary, Banbury, Oxfordshire.

The seat cushions and panels designed by the late Guy Barton form a lesson in the use of colour and stitches to give a rich decorative effect. If you have the chance, do look at the choir stalls in Lancaster Priory.

Colours need to be selected in the church, with the normal lighting used for services. Colours can look quite different under different lights, and what seems harmonious at home under tungsten lighting can look garish and crude under fluorescent lights. Dark blues and browns can appear black in artificial light, and olive greens look brown – so do check before you order lots of wool.

Colours can have meaning as well as beauty. In Christ Church Cathedral, Montreal, they chose a colour scheme both for its religious significance and its suitability. Red stands for sovereign power, so they chose it for their background colour and because a Cathedral bye-law required pew holders in former days, when decorating their pews, to use red as the major colour. They also chose gold as a symbol of pure light; white for innocence and holiness of life, and grey for humility. (See also *Christian symbols*.)

Canvas

Next consider the size of the canvas you are proposing to use, as well as the experience of your workers. At Hampstead we used 16 single (or mono) canvas, and worked the stitches over two threads, making eight stitches to the inch. Even this was too fine for some people, and a few worked on double canvas of about five stitches to the inch. Using such a coarse canvas as this limits the design, which needs to be kept simple, with the minimal amount of detail or shading.

It is well worth while to try out a small sample of a design in the colours you plan to use and on several different sizes of canvas, so that you can assess the effect, not only of the canvas, but also of the way the colours work together. Do look at all these in the church as well.

Using 16 single canvas has the advantage that specific areas which call for fine detail can be worked over one thread. I worked out the designs on graph paper marked in eighths of an inch, convenient for showing the size of the finished kneeler, but the grid on which you draw out a design is a matter of choice, and depends on what is most convenient for the designer and worker. Because our designs were repeated several times, a master drawing was made and copied by the dye-line process in an architectural drawing office. However, there are many new methods of reproducing designs, and it may be that one of these is more economical.

Cut your canvas with ample margins; you will need these when you come to stretch the canvas and make it up. Always buy the best possible, preferably the de luxe quality made with polished thread, which does not tear at your yarn. I have said already that a single or mono canvas gives you more flexibility in the kind of stitches you can use, but there is also a kind called Interlock canvas, adequate but not so strong, which, because of its weave, does not 'give' under tension. Double canvas, sometimes called Penelope, is usually about a count of ten stitches to the inch, although it can be found a little finer, at 12 stitches to the inch. The best canvas used to be made of linen, but nowadays it is cotton.

Wool

A very wide range of colours is found in both the Appleton and Paterna (Paternaya) ranges. These are both stranded wools which give you the option of varying the number of strands used for different stitches; and of course you can have strands of different colours in your needle to give a mottled effect. Tapestry wool and double knitting wool can be used, but they tend to 'pill' and fluff, eventually giving an unfortunate appearance.

Thrums, obtainable from carpet factories, are the waste wool left at the end of the loom when a carpet has been woven. It is quite a coarse wool, very tough, and is cheaper than the finer wools, but you may not be able to match the colours for a repeat order, so make sure you buy enough.

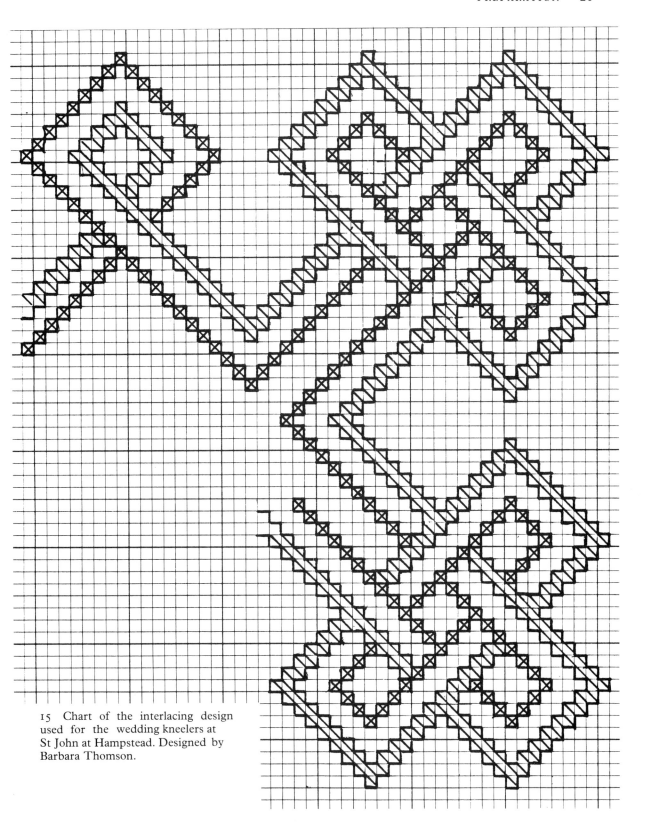

15 Chart of the interlacing design used for the wedding kneelers at St John at Hampstead. Designed by Barbara Thomson.

Working the kneelers

Using a frame

You can work your canvas in the hand, or on a frame, and there are advantages in either method. Frames can be a little unwieldy, and some people are rather scared of using them, but once you get used to it, this can be a very comfortable way of working. You have both hands if the frame is supported, and there are several ways of doing this. The simplest way, of course, is to have a frame on a stand, though that costs more than a frame alone. Or you can have it on a table, with the area you are working on protruding over the edge and held steady by a heavy weight, or a G-clamp. A simple heavy weight is a brick covered with felt or some other thick fabric. A simple frame can be made with the stretchers used for oil paintings, bought from an art supplier (but I find that the wedges supplied get in the way). Many villages have persuaded local handymen to construct frames to which the canvas is stapled or pinned.

It is important to use a frame if you are going to cover a lot of your kneeler with any of the

diagonal types of stitch, such as half cross, tent, jacquard or Byzantine; these stiches, done in the hand, tend progressively to pull the canvas out of true, and you end up with a diamond shape instead of an oblong. It is a question of tensions. Possibly a very experienced worker could do these stitches without trouble, but, for the majority, it is better to play safe and use a frame. A canvas that is badly misshapen by that sort of tension will never be satisfactory; despite several stretchings, the canvas will revert to its diamond shape and will not make up properly; you will find you have a twisted kneeler that will not lie flat. So if you are working the canvas in the hand, avoid this type of stitch, and keep to cross, rice, long leg, gobelin, florentine, and other 'square' stitches.

To stretch a canvas

You will need:

1 A large flat board, such as an old drawing board.
2 An old towel, or several sheets of blotting paper.
3 Large mapping pins or drawing pins (thumb tacks). I prefer the mapping pins: they have

16   Work in a frame.

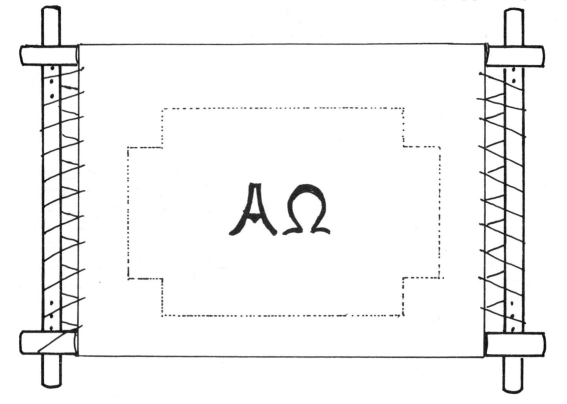

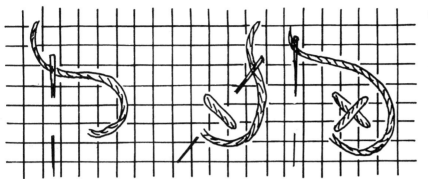

cross stitch

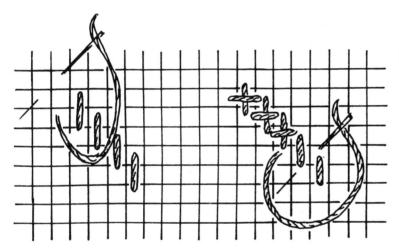

upright cross stitch

gobelin stitch

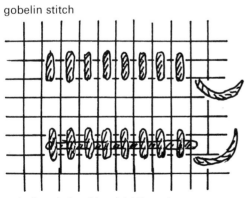

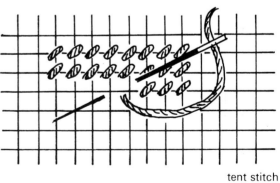

gobelin stitch with a laid thread

tent stitch

17 Useful stitches.

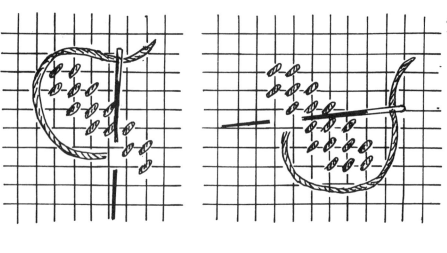

alternative method of
working tent stitch

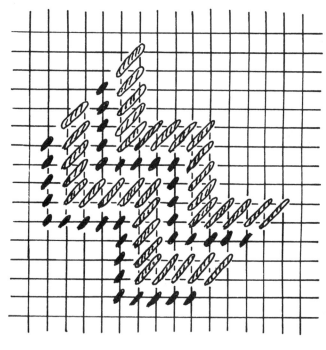

jacquard stitch

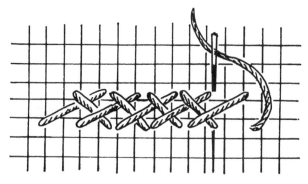

long leg cross stitch

plaited gobelin stitch

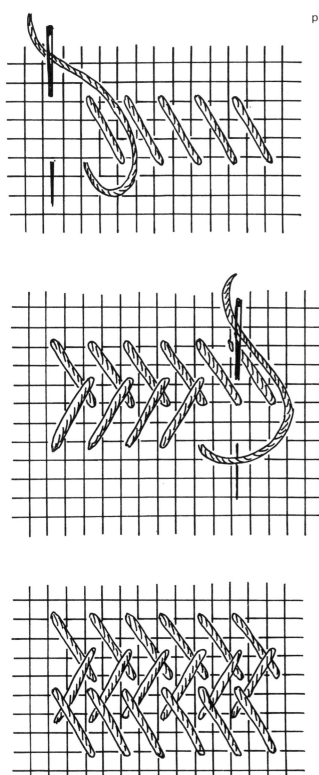

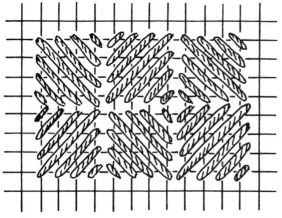

cushion stitch

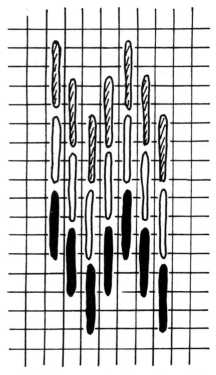

florentine stitch

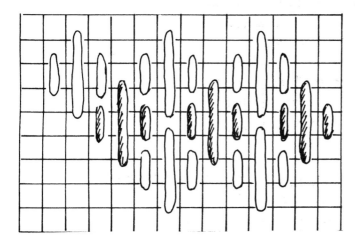

Hungarian stitch

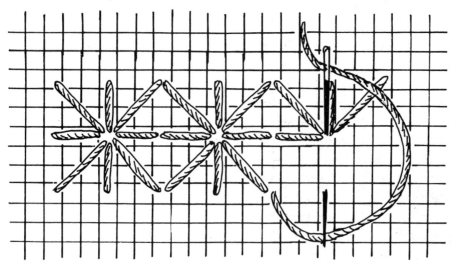

eyelet or star stitch

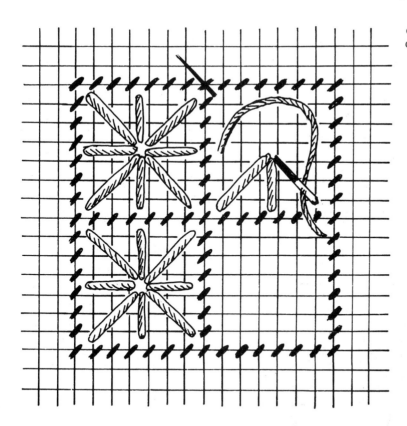

eyelet or star stitch
on a squared ground

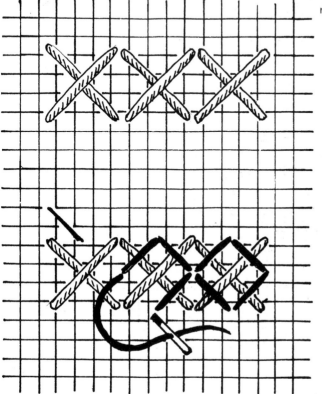

rice stitch, or crossed corners

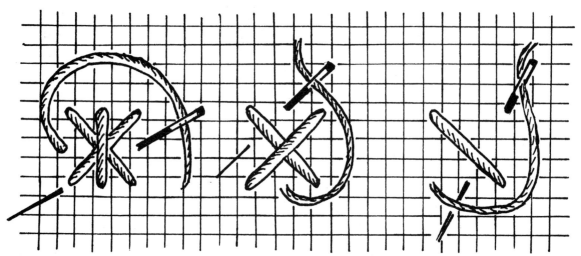

Smyrna stitch

bigger heads and longer pins and are thus easier to hold and to insert and remove.

4 A tape measure, and/or a T-square.

Lay the towel over the board, and pin down with flat pins. If textured stitches have been used, you may find that a double layer of towelling gives a better result.

Lay the canvas face down on top of the towelling, one end parallel with the edge of the board, and pin this down – through the canvas, not through the worked area. Pull the canvas straight, and pin the other end in a similar fashion, ensuring that you have pulled it as tight as possible. Then treat the other two sides in a similar way, pulling the canvas until it is quite taut and straight. You may find that you have to adjust the pins. When certain that it is taut, straight and square, soak the canvas with water, using a sponge or cloth, making sure that you have wetted all the worked canvas. Leave this for 24–48 hours to dry thoroughly and naturally – do not put it in the airing cupboard or in front of the fire, and *never* press with a hot iron.

When the canvas is thoroughly dry, remove the pins and lift it off, and you will find it lovely and smooth, with any textured stitches standing out as they should, especially if you have used towelling rather than blotting paper.

Making-up

If you are going to make up the kneelers yourself, it is important to do the work in a profes-
sional way. If you know anyone who has had classes in upholstery, pick their brains, or persuade them to give you and your team lessons on how to do it. Remember that a kneeler takes a lot of weight. This puts a strain on the canvas and the wool, which must be properly supported. After spending many hours working on the embroidery, you do not want it to be spoiled in use and to wear out years sooner than it should, because the stuffing is not good enough. A good firm foam is normally employed and must be obtained from a specialist source: it is unlikely that you will find it in an ordinary high street shop. Reconstituted foam no. 5 is recommended; at Hampstead we used this, but I had the pads cut one inch wider in both directions, and half an inch deeper, than the embroidery. This means that the kneelers are under tension, and now, almost 20 years later, they still look as good as new. In time, foam pads start to disintegrate, so many people cover them in fabric such as calico before inserting them into the kneelers. Disintegration of the foam is accelerated by heat, but in most churches this is unlikely to be a major problem.

Filling

At Mulbarton, a village $5\frac{1}{2}$ miles from Norwich, the kneelers are firm and strong. Only the top is embroidered. After careful research it was decided to make up the filling as follows:

Underneath the canvas:
One piece of carpet felt.

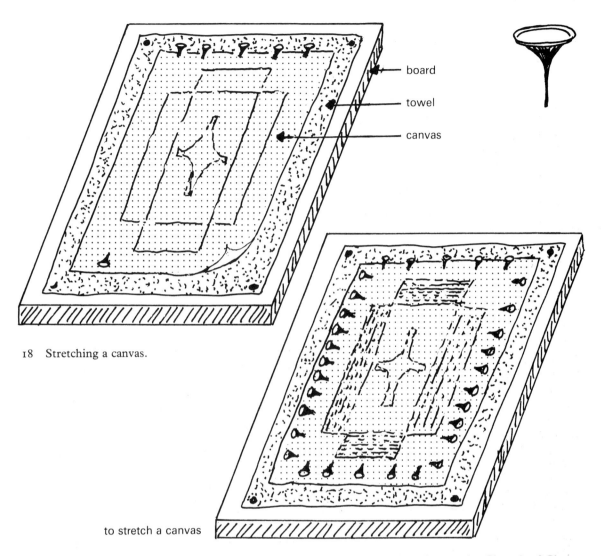

board

towel

canvas

18   Stretching a canvas.

to stretch a canvas

One piece of reconstituted plastic foam of 2.5 kg (5 lb) density, 30.5 × 23 × 2.5 cm (12 × 9 × 1 in.). This is bonded to:

One piece of reconstituted plastic foam of 4 kg (9 lb) density, 30.5 × 23 × 7.5 cm (12 × 9 × 3 in.)

One piece of beige-coloured Lionide, a durable cloth-backed vinyl (which also covers the sides).

One piece of 9 mm plywood 29 × 20 cm (11½ × 8 in.). This is stuck with PVA adhesive to the base of the pad.

Two battens 2.5 cm (1 in.) wide 'D' moulding 17.5 cm (7 in.) long, screwed into the outside of the base.

By bulk purchase of materials, the cost of each of the 94 kneelers was kept down to £6.40.

For the altar kneelers at the Church of Christ the Servant, Bristol, the filling is both spiritual and practical. Prayers by members of the congregation, written on linen, were inserted between the pad and the wadding.

Horse hair from old mattresses, nylon stockings, wood chips and shavings are among the filling materials we heard about. At St Pancras, Kingston, East Sussex, they sent their kneelers to an upholsterer who used wood chips and horse hair. Result: they lost their shape and so have now been refitted with foam blocks.

At Christ Church, Chesham, Buckinghamshire, they stiffened their kneelers by placing a light backing of 6 mm (⅕ in.) plywood inside the lining. This was done by a parishioner who was an experienced carpenter.

(a)

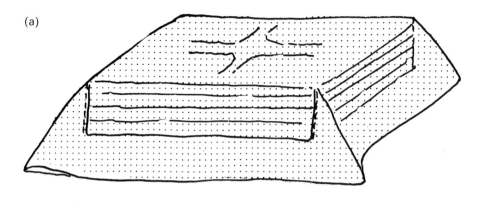

(b)

(c)

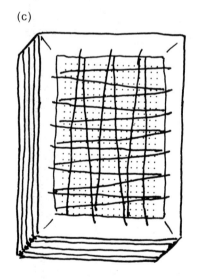

(d)

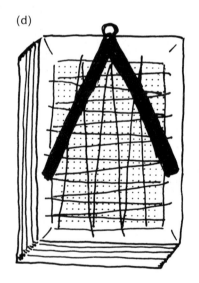

19 Methods of making-up. (a) Turn canvas to wrong side and backstitch corners. (b) Turn cover to right side; corners can now be oversewn. (c) Lace the canvas over the pad. (d) Attach the hanging ring with webbing stitched down on the canvas. Finally, cover the base with glazed hessian or vinyl.

At St Finnbarr, Dornoch, Sutherland, they are using their old kneelers for fillings. These, with the addition of nylon stockings, are made into pads to fit an outer cover (of any suitably strong material). The base is made of Irish crash.

For years the staff of Shawnigan Lake School, Vancouver Island, collected nylon stockings for filling the kneelers they were making for the school chapel. According to Mrs. M. M. McBean, who took part in the project, 'some loving soul stitched them into neat rectangles'.

Whatever your filling, you should keep in mind the purpose of kneelers and make them comfortable to use. This is not so obvious as it sounds. Some have knobbly designs which, however beautiful to look at, are hard on the knees.

20 The mosaic floor of the village church of Orta in Northern Italy was the inspiration for this design by Barbara Thomson for the Church of St John at Hampstead.

Display

We hung our Hampstead kneelers on hooks so that they were out of the way when not in use and the floor could be cleaned easily. But because they hung freely, it became a strong temptation to small children to use them as swings when bored with the service – this did a lot of damage. When the church is redecorated we plan to raise them so that they hang from immediately below the prayer-book shelf where they will be less vulnerable. The church is used for concerts and plays, and the kneelers will be less in the way on these occasions, as well, if they are kept higher up.

If you are going to hang them, it is advisable to support the ring, or rings, by a heavy tape or webbing, so that the weight of the kneeler is not all on the canvas. (See fig. 19.)

The hanging of kneelers within the pews offers a problem; after a time hooks bend or

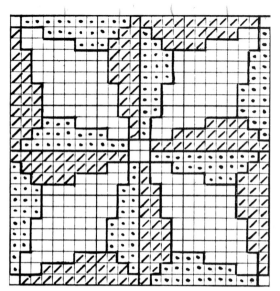

21 Chart of the pattern for the Orta kneeler (see fig. 20).

break. Mary Loveband, in charge of the kneeler scheme at St Mary the Virgin, Wimbledon, solved her problem by persuading a local iron-monger to present the church with 400 large brass hooks ('no cup hooks for us!'). These add to the pleasing effect and are practically indes-tructible.

Some pews have strategically placed ledges which eliminate the need for hooks and allow the kneelers to be seen as one enters the church. At St Nicholas, Thames Ditton, Surrey, the kneelers fit tightly between the shelf at the top of the pew and the ledge (made by John Kerr, the organizer's husband). At All Saints, Steep, Hampshire, the plainness of the interior con-trasts sharply with the kneelers, especially as their backgrounds of dark and light blue are alternated, according to Canon Douglas Snelgar, the designer, 'to give a three-dimensional effect'.

In All Hallows, Upper Dean, Bedfordshire, the kneelers hang by multi-coloured plaited wool sewn into a corner. Surprisingly, this sim-ple device has lasted for ten years without fray-ing.

At Holy Trinity, Stratford-upon-Avon, which has an impressive series based on the words and pictures suggested in the *Benedicite*, they decided to hang the kneelers horizontally so that the name of the object on the side and the picture on the front could be seen together. Because the 800 kneelers in St Clement Danes, London, hang vertically, the choice of design is

necessarily restricted. This must have been frus-trating.

Sometimes you will see kneelers of different sizes in a church. This will usually mean that they are old kneelers which have been recovered; but in one church the different depths are inten-tional. This is at St Lawrence-in-the-Square, Winchester, where the deeper kneelers are for members of the congregation who have diffi-culty in getting up from shallower ones.

Know-how

If in your parish you have no-one experienced enough to take charge and to instruct, the very thought of a kneeler project can be daunting. There are ways out, however. In St Mary-at-Latton the embroidery group was just large enough to allow it to become affiliated to the Essex Handicraft Association. This was of im-mense help. At Thames Ditton, the organizer, Mavis Kerr, and other members of the congre-gation, were, or had been, students at Hampton School of Needlework. The staff there gave advice and encouragement, as well as supplying materials.

We have come across examples of totally inex-perienced embroiderers who have made per-fectly acceptable kneelers. For example, at Exeter Cathedral the designs for kneelers in the nave – birds and flowers of the West Country – appealed widely, and offers of help rushed in both from experts and from those who 'needed a great deal of tuition, even on how to thread a needle with wool', as Winifred Lockwood re-cords in her booklet on the Cathedral embroid-ery.

Help has come from many sources. One small parish found it in the needlework shop of a neighbouring town. Artists, designers, and teachers have been called in. At Great Bealings, Suffolk, Moss Fuller, an artist with local connec-tions, made coloured sketches followed by scale drawings.

Book illustrations have inspired kneeler schemes. At St Luke, Endon, Staffordshire, they took their design from *Saints, Signs, and Sym-bols* (SPCK), enlarging the illustrations. Workers in the congregation of St Kieran, Campbeltown, Argyllshire, got most of their ideas from Coats' *Church Kneelers*, No. 1058, though they could fit only a part of any of the designs on their small kneelers.

Funding

On Monday afternoons kneeler-makers gather at The Admiral's House, Hingham, in Norfolk. They have been doing so since 1969. Numbers vary from ten to twelve in the winter to six or seven in the summer. Because St Andrew, Hingham, the second largest parish church in the county, has needed costly repairs, they felt they should be independent of other fund-raising efforts, so everyone pays 12p for tea and biscuits provided by the hostess, Joy Hare. This money has almost covered the cost of materials for the 300 kneelers already completed.

The Friends of Exeter Cathedral provide generous financial help annually, and individual donations come from 'people who admire the

22 (*Below*) One of the altar rail kneelers for Winchester Cathedral, designed by Guy Barton, with the Coronation of the Virgin in the central medallion.

23 (*Foot of page*) Detail of the medallion from fig. 22.

work'. The Winchester Friends paid for the nave altar kneelers in the Cathedral, and many other 'Friends' have supported kneeler schemes. But in small country parishes seeking to raise money for materials which can cost a great deal, it is usually a matter of coffee-mornings in the vicarage (as at Long Compton, Warwickshire). Often money is given for a kneeler worked in memory of a member of the family or a friend. Economies are practised, such as the use of 'thrums' (waste material from carpet manufacturers), though these are more suitable for coarse canvas. Making up kneelers, if professionally managed, is expensive. At many churches it is done by parishioners, or even embroiderers themselves, and is an arduous task. Christ Church, Woking, and many others, do their own making-up.

Two-thirds of the money for the kneelers at St Mary, Great Bealings, Suffolk, was raised by personal sponsoring, and the rest from one large fund-raising event. The kneelers now make money for church funds through the sale of a

well-illustrated booklet which includes practical details of materials, stitches, choice of colours, stretching and making up. As Cynthia Brown, author of this excellent little book, puts it: 'Being able to stretch and make up the canvases in the village saved a considerable sum of money.'

At Thriplow, a Cambridgeshire village of fewer than 500 inhabitants, they have their own way of raising money. Once a year, in spring, they hold a 'daffodil weekend' which has become so well known that people come from long distances to see the thousands of daffodils, craft work made locally, the church, the old houses, and the smithy. One year they made £7,000; the money goes toward the upkeep of the church, the school, the cricket club, the Over Sixties club, and church kneelers.

The idea of 'giving' a kneeler has helped to pay for materials in many parishes. At St Mary and St Milburgh, Offenham, Worcestershire, when old kneelers had to be replaced, parishioners and others were persuaded to pay for new ones in memory of relations or friends. At St Peter, Allerton, West Yorkshire, they bought canvas, hessian, and compressed latex very

24 Kneeler from Thriplow, showing the Manor House with the daffodils out in the spring.

cheaply, or received these materials free. At the start, in 1975, they used four-ply carpet wool of the required shade of red until this ran out and could not be repeated; then they got hold of carpet wool in a natural colour which an embroiderer's husband (in the trade) had dyed. These economies meant that they were able to complete 200 kneelers for £1.50 each. (It must be added that these are only two inches deep because they rest on kneeler rails which are raised about six inches from the floor.)

At St Luke, Endon, Staffordshire, a group made 186 items, including 164 nave kneelers, three altar kneelers, two sanctuary kneelers, two for the vicar's and curate's stalls, three for the prayer desk, and one wedding kneeler, for £339.40. Of this, the church paid £200, and the rest came from donations. At St Mary, Fordingbridge, Hampshire, they met the cost of their kneeler project, including 75 for the nave and 30 for the Lady Chapel, by gifts of wool and various small events.

Many kneelers are sent away to be filled and, if necessary, upholstered. The jobs, if done 'at home', obviously cost much less; professional filling varies in price. At St Peter and St Paul, Long Compton, Warwickshire, their kneelers – of which only the tops were embroidered – were filled, and the sides and base covered in fabric-backed vinyl for only £1 each.

By far the most detailed account of funding we have come across is that of the Wakefield Cathedral project which began in 1980 when Marie Cooke, a final year student at Bretton Hall College, offered to design the kneelers as part of her course. It was at once agreed to accept her offer, and to launch the scheme as part of the Centenary Development Programme, Provost Lister produced an advance of £250. Mrs Cooke proved to be able to get favourable terms for the materials. In all, 500 kneelers were wanted; the materials cost £2,415.58, and printing, stationery, and postage, £149.89. After charging embroiderers £7 per pack, they made a profit of £368.57: money that went towards buying some essential items for the Cathedral.

Not every project is so successful. Some never start because they are felt to be too expensive. At St Mary, Farnham Royal, Buckinghamshire, they decided instead to buy standard kneelers to replace disintegrating kneeling mats.

At St Mary, Wimbledon, embroiderers are encouraged to use home-made frames which can be supplied for £2.50, much cheaper than at a shop. At Abbots Ann, Hampshire, a kind friend made and gave the frames.

The communal benefits of kneeler projects are clearly shown by an example from St Andrew's Episcopal Church, Hopkinton Village, New Hampshire, USA. There, in 1975, women of the congregation began to look for something to replace their annual Christmas Fair so that they could get back to their weekly meetings. The church was about to celebrate its 150th year when Mrs Thomas Thompson came to live in Hopkinton. Formerly the owner of a needlework shop in Alabama, and a lecturer and teacher, she suggested that they should discard their faded altar kneelers and make new ones. This was the project they were looking for. They formed a Needlework Guild, attended a talk with coloured slides on church embroidery in England, and organized weekly workshops where they could practise stitches. Eighteen months later they had finished 14 kneelers and five cushions in original designs for the sanctuary.

How had they paid for the materials? They needed more than $1,000. They launched the scheme with $800 they had in hand from selling cookery books; they invited donations; and they announced that individual kneelers could be purchased, and that on these a memorial plaque in *petit point* would be attached. (See also *Crosses*.)

On 14 April 1985, 36 communion kneelers were dedicated at Bethany United Methodist Church, Houston, Texas, USA. To pay for the project, members of the Altar Guild organized a series of fund-raising events: luncheons, sale of Christmas cards, a flea market, and envelope-filling. In this way they made $4,000, to which the congregation added $2,400. Before the first stitch was on canvas the total cost of $8,000 was in sight. Many kneelers were given in memory of relations or friends, or to honour living members of families.

Let Faith Hanna have the last word on funding. She had urged the women at Grace Episcopal Church, Winfield, Kansas, USA, to get on with the needlepoint they had been talking about for years, and members subscribed for 'in memoriam' kneelers. All the same, she said, 'It was staggering to purchase $100 worth of yarn at one time.' (See also *Christian symbols*.)

Disasters and triumphs

Most of this book is about triumphs; as the pictures prove, kneeler design can be immensely worth while. Even in tiny communities, groups have achieved sets of kneelers that add to the beauty of the church; but it must be said that things can go wrong. We have heard of organizers being let down and forced to give up before they started. One organizer, involved in a complex scheme, admitted that one of her workers had kept a kneeler for eight years and had not finished it. (Not quite a disaster, but she must wonder if it will ever be done.) There are tales of kneelers that disappear, or of half-completed kneelers that come back to base and must be unpicked. A dog ate one, and at the same place another failed to return when its embroiderer ran away with the chauffeur! One experienced needleworker joined a scheme and suffered from the bad designs offered to her. 'They were,' she said, 'more suitable for a drawing-room than a church, and they used cheap wool which broke frequently.'

One needlepointer from the Church of the Good Samaritan, Villa Nova, Pennsylvania, left her work on a train and it was never recovered.

Others from this church took theirs on vacation, and heat and humidity made the ink used to paint the design on the canvas fade irrevocably.

But successes far outnumber failures. At St John, Woking, Surrey, the organizer, Mick Tapling, confesses that they started with more enthusiasm than knowledge. 'We wanted,' she says, 'the Seven Days of Creation round the chancel rails, and felt that this gave us scope ... There are many original designs of varying degrees of excellence. We are very proud of them; they are all our own work and not designed by experts.'

In another Surrey parish, at the small country church of St John the Baptist, Puttenham, they made and designed the kneelers themselves, starting in 1970 when the Revd John Rose-Casemore, Rector at the time, suggested the scheme and agreed to organize it. 'We know,' the embroiderers say, 'that compared with the beautiful kneelers in some churches they aren't very good, but we like them and we enjoyed the experience of working together.'

Underlying Wakefield's kneeler project instruction, 'If for any reason you are unable to finish the kneeler please return it to the Cathedral personally or by post,' there is, surely, a history of lost canvases!

25   Mickey Mouse, for the children at St John's, Woking, Surrey.

PART TWO

○·

Inspirations

Kneeling ne'er spoil'd silk stockings.
(George Herbert)

He was wrong. Torn and leaking kneelers have ruined many a pair of nylons. At St Martin, Epsom, Surrey, they started kneeler making 'partly to get people together and partly because the Rexine covering was causing so many casualties to nylon tights'.

Not all kneeler projects began because the old kneelers had disintegrated. St John the Evangelist, Farnham Common, in Buckinghamshire, started theirs to celebrate the church's Jubilee in 1967; at St Luke, Endon, Staffordshire, they looked for ideas that would engage the time and talents of women of the congregation. With a group of 12 they began their seven years' task of making 186 pieces of needlework (a sum that covers, apart from the kneelers, the Bishop's chair cushion, cushions for the clergy's stalls and the choir, and two offertory bags).

In this section of the book we look at the reasons why many successful kneeler projects were begun, and the subjects which inspired their varied themes.

Abstract designs

Virginia Woolf once wrote: 'A story-telling picture is as pathetic and ludicrous as a trick played by a dog.' She would probably have felt the same about story-telling in canvas work (although, as we show in this book, we should not have agreed with her).

To get right away from story-telling, the abstract design is the answer, and there are some strong examples. They give plenty of scope in both colour schemes and stitchery. For Southwark Cathedral, on the south bank of the Thames, George Pace, its consulting architect, produced an arrangement of blocks of colours in various shapes inside a dark red framework. Members of the congregation and people from the diocese, who worked the kneelers, could use the colours in whatever way they liked, but they had to use all of them.

The same style of kneeler, with a blue background, also designed by Pace, fills the long nave of St Albans Abbey, Hertfordshire. Following this system, squares, rectangles, ovals and arcs could be worked in a combination of green, dark blue, cerise, pale beige and lilac; or yellow, darker beige, crimson and orange; or crimson, yellow, beige and bright blue.

Chelmsford Cathedral, Essex, has some new kneelers in abstract designs by the distinguished embroiderer, Beryl Dean; Belinda, Lady Montagu, designed a 30 foot long altar kneeler for Salisbury Cathedral, Wiltshire, taking colours from the modern east window. Members of the Sarum Group worked it in a number of different stitches. Like the altar kneelers in St Mary's Cathedral, Edinburgh, these variations on crosses are treated in an abstract style.

The fact that every one of these abstract designs comes from a cathedral is probably significant. Perhaps designers feel that they are better suited to such large buildings.

Antiques

In the past, mice, moths, and wear and tear demolished kneelers thoroughly if not rapidly. Thus there are few antique kneelers in existence. In 50 or so years the kneelers of our day will have grown old, but although many will be well preserved (moth-proofing and professional filling will have seen to that), they will not have soared in value. There will be too many of them.

26 Chelmsford Cathedral: kneeler designed by Beryl Dean.

27 Another of Beryl Dean's designs for Chelmsford Cathedral.

The Victoria & Albert Museum has one kneeler, dated 1700, on show. Made of woollen velvet (probably manufactured in the Netherlands), it comes from Langley Church, in Buckinghamshire. Even more interesting is the set of five red leather kneelers (dated 1796) which is still used at the altar of the Georgian church at Mildenhall, near Marlborough, Wiltshire. (John Betjeman said that as you enter you walk into a Jane Austen novel.) To preserve them, these precious antiques were taken to pieces and filled with a special plastic, the guide-book explains. It adds, very reasonably, 'We have been told they are unique. They were too brittle to stitch properly.' It is good to think that they are particularly treasured, for the history of the site begins with medieval times, and possibly earlier.

With commendable enterprise, in October 1984, the church of St John the Baptist in the Wilderness, Cragg Vale, near Hebden Bridge, Yorkshire, organized a Festival of Kneelers. Among the exhibits were some that go back 'at least to the 1890s'. They belong to the Cragg Vale church and to All Saints, Dewsbury. Also in the Festival was a Cragg Vale kneeler from the 1920s, noted in the catalogue as better than those from the 1890s 'but less durable'.

28　The Agnus Dei on a kneeler in the church of St Peter and St Paul, Kirton, near Boston, Lincolnshire. Worked in tent and rice stitch on a green ground.

In St Nicholas, Great Bookham, Surrey, they possess an altar kneeler which came to them from Slyfield Chapel. (There are brasses in the church for fifteenth- and sixteenth-century Slyfields.) The altar kneeler is now nearly 50 years old, and is typical of the canvas work of its time. Though hardly an antique, it is a contemporary of the Winchester kneelers which started the movement.

Christian symbols

Christian symbols are not always welcomed on kneelers; in the Lutheran Church they are not allowed. But certainly, they lend themselves effectively to canvas work design. For three side-altar kneelers at Christ Church, Chesham, Buckinghamshire, they are worked in a well-spaced arrangement upon a blue background in a balanced selection of colours. A sacred monogram, the Chi Rho (for Christ) is in yellow and light blue with a crimson cross; the fleur-de-lys on either side is in pale grey and lemon; and the chalice, in chequered grey and white, has a red diamond on the stem. Because the total length required would have been cumbersome to work in one piece, it was divided into three, each with

29   St Mary's Cathedral, Glasgow: effective design of a crown worked on canvas with five stitches to the inch, on a blue ground.

30   Dove carrying a leaf, at St Genewys, Scotton, Lincolnshire. Worked on canvas with five stitches to the inch, in Parisian stitch, rice stitch, and cross stitch. The colours are reds and black.

identical designs (by Ethel Stevens, who worked one of them herself), so that they are interchangeable. This shows forethought, as the central kneeler gets more wear.

Using bright colours on navy blue, a group of embroiderers joined together to make two altar kneelers for a side chapel in the Priory Church of St Lawrence, Snaith, in Humberside. The design consists of symbols including the chalice, Cross, fish, flames of the Holy Spirit, and Alpha and Omega. Modern Christian symbols for the Year of the Child, and the Cross in the boat for the Ecumenical Year, decorate the wider kneelers for the main altar.

The four corner kneelers at the altar of Bethany United Methodist Church, Houston, Texas, symbolize the Creation, the Exodus, the Resurrection and the Church. In all, 36 kneelers were made, and dedicated in April, 1985. Joann Roach organized the scheme.

31 Lincoln Cathedral depicted on a kneeler in the Morning Chapel of the Cathedral. Worked in long leg, tent, rice, gobelin, eyelet, cushion and cross stitch.

The Lamb and Flag (or, as it is sometimes known, Banner) symbol of the Resurrection, appears frequently: in rice and tent stitches at St Peter and St Paul, Kirton, near Boston, Lincs; at St Mary the Virgin, Oxenhope, Yorkshire; and at St Mary, Elland, Yorkshire, where a kneeler was dedicated to Father Clifford Green on the twentyfifth anniversary of his priesthood. In St Pancras, Kingston, Sussex, kneelers were embroidered with symbols in shades of yellow on a blue ground. At St Peter, Rodmell, Sussex, they have similar designs worked in red, blue, and yellow. Here they started off with homespun wool dyed with cochineal, woad, and golden rod. Louisa Pesel would have approved.

In Sir George Gilbert Scott's Cathedral of St Mary the Virgin, Glasgow, the kneeler project began in 1966 under the leadership of Ruth MacIntosh, wife of the Provost, the Very Revd Hugh MacIntosh, with Evelyn Ward as organizer. By 1972 over 500 had been completed, many with early Christian and Celtic symbols; designs of crosses, fish, ship, rose and moon came from Coats' *Church Kneelers*, and were

worked in cross stitch on double thread canvas (five to the inch). Evelyn Ward designed the vine leaves, dove, cruse, and the crown of the Madonna, using single thread canvas (ten to the inch) with crewel and tapestry wools. Only the tops were embroidered, with vinyl sides and bases. Reds, blues, and greens predominate for the backgrounds.

At St Genewys, Scotton, Lincolnshire, they have dove and cross designs on coarse canvas, and at St Peter, Elmsett, Suffolk, there are some religious symbols worked mainly in cross stitch on double canvas (seven to the inch) in russet red, black, white, yellow, and olive green.

Each of the eight designs (for 167 kneelers) at St Anne, Moseley, Birmingham, is worked in the same colour scheme: shades of red, blue and black. All are Christian symbols, including the dove, the fish, the crown of thorns, a hammer and nails, the Pentecostal fire and Chi Rho. Help in preparing the scheme came from the staff at Bournville School of Art.

The needlepoint altar kneeler at Christ Church Cathedral, Montreal, is not the first to lie there. In 1904 the Chancel Guild and girls of the Women's Auxiliary made some; these original kneelers – one is preserved in the sacristy – were replaced in 1956 by three needlepoint cushions worked by 30 church members. Now repaired, they have been relegated to the Chapel of St John of Jerusalem, and the new kneeler, made of more lasting modern materials, was dedicated in 1978.

After much discussion it was agreed that traditional symbolic designs would be best for a building which is nineteenth-century Gothic. Designed by Mrs George Brickenden, an artist and needlepointer, the work was carried out by members of the congregation, most of whom had no previous experience of needlepointing. (Thirty small canvases, painted with designs, were used in teaching.) The completed kneeler, which is 27 feet long with nearly a million stitches, contains 17 panels done separately and joined together by hand; 14 members, working in pairs, successfully achieved 'mirror images'. The backgrounds, and most of the designs, are in basket-weave stitch on French canvas in Paternaya Persian wool.

Symbols used are the descending dove with three-rayed nimbus for the Holy Spirit; wheat for the body of Christ; grapes for the blood of Christ; the crown for Our Lord's kingly office, eternal life and victory over sin and death; the fleur-de-lys for the Holy Trinity; the open book for the Word of God; the lily for its connection with the Annunciation; the bee for activity, diligence, work and good order, also for sweetness and religious eloquence; the beehive for a pious and unified community; the oak as a symbol of Christ and Christian endurance against adversity; and the butterfly as a symbol of the Resurrection of Christ.

The border is copied from a flower design carved into the altar steps. As the author of a booklet from Montreal adds: 'An exciting moment came when it was discovered that, where these flowers linked, a cross miraculously appeared.'

The needlepointers of St Simon-on-the-Sound, Fort Walton Beach, Florida, took just over a year to complete their kneelers ('Some husbands did a stitch or two', Patricia M. Thornber says). They are symbolic seascapes: how, in a church with this address, could they be otherwise? The shells are the kind found in the nearby Gulf of Mexico, and the curling waves, shaded from white to pale blue, also belong to the Gulf. Among the waves three fish swim in a circle to represent the Trinity; an anchor cross stands as a centre piece on another wave kneeler, and Alpha and Omega are on another. A row of plain gold crosses runs along the dark green sides; the acolytes have kneelers decorated with angels in trailing robes on pale blue grounds, and, in darker blue lettering, 'O ye Waters of the Firmament, Bless ye the Lord,' and 'Even the Winds of the Sea Obey Him.' Nothing could be more fitting for Fort Walton Beach. (See also *Modern churches*.)

A Green Man looks out with sparkling eyes from kneelers at St Mary the Virgin, Great Shelford, Cambridgeshire. No wonder, for this is the head of the Green Man who, wreathed in foliage (oak or hawthorn, usually) acted his own death and then came to life. He is a Christian symbol of the Resurrection found frequently on bosses, misericords and other church carvings, and here, in Great Shelford, on kneelers worked in brick, long leg, tent and Hungarian stitches in blue, greens and yellow. Only the tops are embroidered; the sides are made of blue velvet, and they have a firm base with little rubber feet.

Seven years ago members of St Monica's Guild of St Michael and All Angels, Kelowna, British Columbia, started to meet weekly to make altar linens, vestments, banners, and also chancel rail kneelers, completed in 1980. The

32 The Green Man, from St Mary the Virgin, Great Shelford. Blue ground with central panel in gold brick stitch. The Green Man himself is in several shades of green tent stitch, with glittering lurex eyes.

needlepoint design consists, simply, of angels on a crimson background, and, at the centre, two angels, the Cross and flame. There are three kneelers, each seven feet long. The church itself was built of stone in 1911 when the old wooden building became inadequate.

A collectors' piece for students of Anglo-Saxon architecture, All Saints, Earls Barton, Northamptonshire, has a sturdy tower ornamented with long-and-short quoins and vertical pilaster strips. Inside, there are encircled consecration crosses, said to be a defence against devils. If you wish to light the chancel you put money in the slot-meter. The 250 kneelers in this most unusual setting have a sun at the centre surrounded by a symmetrical design in grey. In the corners the motifs are a tongue of fire, three rings linked together, a five-cornered star, and a moon. All four are worked in gold on either dark green, dark blue, or maroon backgrounds.

When Dorothy Harris, who designed the kneelers, died, her husband asked for a memorial to be placed in the church. With this in mind, Diane Bettles designed and worked for the prayer-desk a kneeler to complement others in the church. It has a Roman cross in the centre, a white rose on either side, and a frame made up of needlework scissors laid end to end.

Probably, when we think of Coventry Cathedral, restored after the wartime blitz, we recall John Piper's glass or Graham Sutherland's tapestry of the risen Christ, but it also has 1,000 kneelers designed by Sir Basil Spence and Anthony Blee. One of them contains the Cross, the fish in the circle of eternity, and an outer circle that illustrates the gift of tongues; on another, an elongated dove (for the Holy Spirit) glides above the waters of baptism. Worked chiefly in tent stitch, these come from every parish in the diocese. They have black cross stitch borders; the colours for the tops are blue, mauves and green, and, for the sides, yellow, greens and mauve.

Some less familiar symbols were chosen for kneelers at St Lawrence, Effingham, Surrey. Designed by Joan Bedale and Jessica Page, they include the catacomb fish which goes back to the persecution of the early Christians; the lion of Judah; the great anchor (from the Greek); the fish and clover (a Trinity symbol taken from the *English Hymnal* cover); and the phoenix (for the Resurrection). There are many others. For example, Elizabeth Blair designed and worked an

33   The catacomb fish, designed by Joan Bedale for St Lawrence, Effingham.

Elizabethan galleon whose mast and trees form a cross; it symbolizes the Church of God.

The Bethlehem Chapel in the crypt of the National Cathedral in Washington, DC, contains 200 kneelers based on Nativity emblems; and, in the chapel dedicated to Joseph of Arimathea, there are four fixed kneelers behind the altar rail. Worked in gentle colours, they have a geometrical design of trellises, the crown of thorns, and herbs of remembrance: rosemary, aloes, myrrh, and hyssop.

It was the National Cathedral's needlepoint that gave those in charge at the Church of the Savior, Canton, Ohio, the idea of having kneelers of their own. Nancy Holwick and Betty Prentice devised the central panels (religious symbols), and an artist, Debbie Forsythe, painted the canvases and designed the backgrounds. A carnation is worked on every kneeler because this was President McKinley's favourite flower; he was a prominent member of the church until his assassination in 1901.

For many years, at Grace Episcopal Church, Winfield, Kansas, the women discussed kneelers until, in desperation, Faith Hanna said: 'Let's quit talking about it, and let's do something.' They did; and, within a year, they had a set of altar kneelers with symbols of the four Apostles, and, in the aisle, with the Trinity. The lamb and flag has been worked on the litany desk kneeler. Tent stitch is used throughout, in blue and gold. An 'In memoriam' record in needlepoint hangs in the church.

The chalice, descending dove, open book, lamb and flag, and other symbols decorate the nine altar kneelers at New St Paul's Anglican Church, Woodstock, Ontario. They are at the centre of elongated quatrefoils worked in red and framed in yellow on blue.

The church mouse

Here among long-discarded cassocks,
Damp stools, and half split open hassocks,
Here where the Vicar never looks
I nibble through old service books . . .
(*John Betjeman*)

Kneeler projects have begun for a number of

34 The church mouse that started it all! Designed by Jane Black for All Saints, Ockham, Surrey.

reasons; one of the most common is the appetite of the church mouse. When old kneelers begin to drip their fillings through nibbled holes, something must be done. 'Something' usually means a bonfire of the old and a set of new.

At All Hallows, Upper Dean, in Bedfordshire, they did not discard the moth-eaten and mouse-chewed old kneelers. They made canvas covers in cross stitch, and thus their kneelers are of different shapes and sizes, depending upon the shape and size of the old ones.

They had to produce new kneelers at All Saints, Ockham, Surrey, when a mouse ate holes in the old ones. The culprit should be flattered by an enchanting kneeler designed and worked by Jane Black. At St John the Baptist, Puttenham, Surrey, a mouse got into the vestment case and started nibbling, so they made a kneeler to recall the event.

We have yet to discover an embroidered clothes moth on a kneeler. Although wool is moth-proofed these days, some people are still afraid to use it. At Horsham St Faith, near Norwich, they used nylon 'to combat moths'.

Crosses

If a count were taken we should find that the Cross appears more often than any other symbol on embroidered kneelers. Simple crosses are often effective, although sometimes the mere suggestion of one as part of a design can be even more so. At St Peter and St Paul, that large, lofty church in the ironstone village of Deddington in Oxfordshire, they have many crosses on blue and crimson backgrounds. The late Henry Eyre Crowe drew and worked a descending dove with outstretched wings inside a rounded cross, and at each corner a smaller cross. At St Fillan, Buckstone Park, Edinburgh, the kneelers have very simple crosses with variations in shades of green and blue and a nice selection of stitches. These kneelers, which are only about two inches thick, would be even better if they had a firmer stuffing.

A single cross stretches from side to side of some kneelers at St Mary and All Saints, Beaconsfield, Buckinghamshire. Several small crosses form a pattern on others here. With shaded gold and beige for the larger cross, and striped red, blue or green backgrounds, the stitches make the texture interesting.

Surely the most remote kneelers in the world are at St Christopher on Saturna, in the Cana-

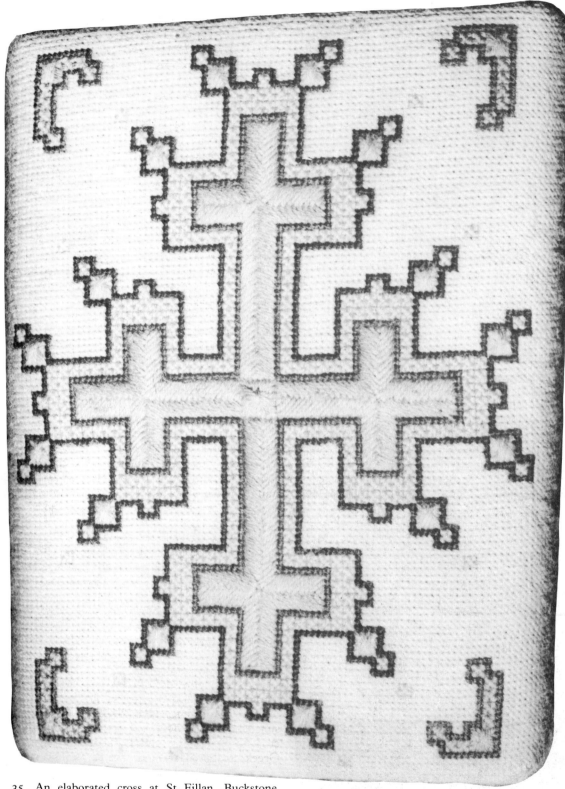

35   An elaborated cross at St Fillan, Buckstone,
Edinburgh.

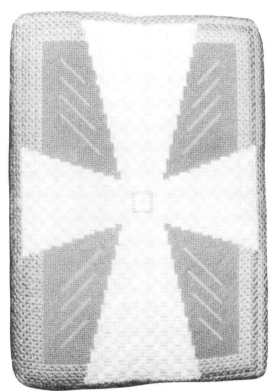

36 A bold cross from St Mary and All Saints, Beaconsfield.

dian State of British Columbia. Saturna, a rocky islet, most southerly of those on the western rim of the stormy Gulf of Georgia between Vancouver Island and the coast of Canada, has a population of under 200. The building of the church, in shape like an upturned boat – a pioneering effort by dedicated local inhabitants – ended in 1972. Materials came from far and wide; timber from a fir tree for the large cross on the west wall was felled on a neighbouring island and originally used for a wharf at the only haven on this inhospitable coast. When the wharf was dismantled, Norman Wilson, largely responsible for the building, bought it for a house he hoped to put up for himself. (He was living in a boat at the time.) Instead, he gave it to the church. As for the glass, when a church in Montreal imported some ruby cathedral glass from Belgium but decided not to use it, it was reshipped safely to Saturna.

Services are held there once a month at 2.15, which allows the minister to arrive on the early afternoon ferry and leave on the 4.30 sailing. Members of the Women's Auxiliary of the neighbouring and more pastoral North Pender Island contributed needlepoint covers with gold crosses on a background of blue, as pads for the hard wooden kneelers.

The chapel of Shawnigan Lake School, Vancouver Island, has a stone floor on which the boys knelt somewhat painfully until the chaplain's wife, Mrs McClelland, encouraged the staff to make kneelers. They worked a simple cross as a centrepiece on a green, blue, maroon or gold background. 'If you felt up to it,' Mrs M. M. McBean, a member of the staff, tells us, 'you could get rather fanciful at the corners with Chi Rho, triangles for the Trinity, the Lamb of God, or a symbolic fish. The boy's name and year went on the side.'

A Jerusalem cross (one large one with four smaller ones between the arms) is worked most beautifully upon a chequered ground on one of the older designs in Chelmsford Cathedral.

Ten pounds of wool and more than a million stitches went into the 14 altar kneelers and five cushions at St Andrews Episcopal Church, Hopkinton, New Hampshire. The kneelers which surround the 18-foot rail have needlepointed crosses: St Andrew's diagonal cross, Maltese, Greek, anchor, Latin and Chi Rho crosses. On

37 Design taken from the carving in the Lady Chapel (dating from the time of Henry VIII), at St Mary and All Saints, Beaconsfield.

38 Jerusalem Cross on a kneeler in Chelmsford Cathedral.

the acolytes' kneelers a field of butterflies represents the Resurrection.

Adaptations of the theme are innumerable. Guy Barton evolved both elaborate and simple crosses with equal success, notably at St Paul, Caton, Lancashire, and Lancaster Priory.

Hands across the sea

In the light and spacious medieval city church of the Holy Sepulchre-without-Newgate (sometimes known as St Sepulchre), we are reminded by its kneelers that John Smith, colonist and soldier, was buried here in 1631. Captured by Indians, he is said to have been rescued by their Princess Pocahontas. Thus we can find on a kneeler a map of Chesapeake Bay (worked by Priscilla Warner of Greenwich, Connecticut, in 1970); a pattern of beads in each corner adds an Indian touch. Smith has a kneeler to himself, as well as another for his map making instruments. His patron, William Herbert, 3rd Earl of Pembroke, 1580–1630, is also commemorated. When Smith returned to England he produced maps and pamphlets to help future North American colonists. (See also *Heraldry* and *Words and music*.)

We discover other transatlantic links on some of the 300 kneelers at the dominating church of St Andrew, Hingham, in mid-Norfolk. Samuel Lincoln, Abraham's ancestor in the direct line,

and a local weaver, sailed for America in 1638; a large contingent from Hingham – including their rector, though he did return home – went too, in search of religious freedom. Their ship, the *Delight*, appears on a kneeler worked by a descendant of one of the colonists who sailed in her; and on another, made in Hingham, Massachusetts, we discover the Old Ship Church which was built there in 1681. The oldest building in the place, it is now a house of worship; it gets its name from the timbers, which are employed like those of a ship.

American visitors to Hingham, 'officially a town, but it feels like a village' (so Mrs Hare, who organizes the kneelers, describes it), are instantly responsive to much in the church, which is the second largest in Norfolk. There is a bust of Lincoln; and, on a kneeler, Man landing on the moon, 'which of course, delights them' (Mrs Hare again). (See also *Heraldry*.)

Visitors from Britain to St James, South Pasadena, California, must be just as pleased to find in needlepoint the voyages of Sir Francis Drake and the Pilgrim Fathers. In this series, imaginative and informative, pictures of those who 'go down to the sea in ships' mark important moments in the history of the Episcopalian Church. The earliest voyage is St Paul's, in a somewhat rudimentary vessel, accompanied here by a map of the Mediterranean, with Italy in the west and Judaea in the east. Next, AD 605, St Augustine's arrival in Britain. When Drake sailed in his handsome flagship, the *Golden Hind*, to San Francisco Bay in 1577 he christened one of the coves 'Drake's Bay' and California as 'Nova Albion'. Affixing his proclamation to a tree, he claimed the land for Elizabeth I and her successors, and held the first Episcopal service there in 1579. During the autumn of 1620, the *Mayflower* left Plymouth with the Pilgrim Fathers aboard. A matter of pride in the States is Samuel Seabury's voyage across the Atlantic to become the first American consecrated as Bishop by the Scottish Church (because the English Church was unwilling to do so); this was in 1784 when the Colonists had just won independence. Hanging near the west door of St Mary's Cathedral, Edinburgh, there is a picture of Seabury's consecration. The last (chronologically) in the Pasadena series shows a paddle steamer, the *Golden Gate*, with William Ingraham Kip, first Protestant Episcopalian Bishop of California, landing at San Diego in 1853.

Rigging, oars, sails, the maps, sea birds, and

1 A selection of kneelers from All Saints, Steep, near Petersfield, designed by the vicar, Canon Douglas Snelgar.

2 'The Coronation of the Virgin', designed for the nave altar rail of Winchester Cathedral by Guy Barton.

3 Trilliums and the scallop shells of St James the Great, designed and worked by Vi Eden Bryan for the altar rail at St James's, Hudson Heights, Jopijo, Quebec.

4 Designed and worked by Mary Hanney for the altar rail at All Saints, Ockham, Surrey.

39 An interlaced Celtic cross in golds on a shaded ground of crimsons and purples, designed by Guy Barton for St Paul's, Caton, Lancashire.

40 Lancaster Priory: kneeler designed by Guy Barton. Worked in gobelin, jacquard, rice, tent and long leg stitches.

41   Saint Augustine's voyage to Britain. One of the altar rail kneelers from St James's Church, South Pasadena, California.

42   The *Mayflower* sails from Plymouth to the New World in search of religious freedom in 1620. From St James's Church, South Pasadena.

43   Samuel Seabury sailed to Scotland to be consecrated the first American Bishop in 1784. St James's Church, South Pasadena.

even a rather hungry fish, are all pictorially satisfying. Mrs Charles Hermin donated these outstanding kneelers in thanksgiving for her mother, Kate Plumb; Josephine Jardine, of the Los Angeles Diocesan Altar Guild, did the necessary research and created the designs.

Heraldry

Coats-of-arms look extremely well in canvas work. At Chelsea Old Church, rebuilt after its destruction in the Blitz of 1941, splendid examples include several versions of the Lion and the Unicorn, and coats-of-arms of royal consorts: among them two of Henry VIII's wives (he was Lord of the Manor), and Queen Charlotte, who had her own Band of Chelsea Volunteers.

Diocesan arms appear on numerous kneelers all over the country. Selectively, we might name two exceptional designs by Jane Black, embroidered by Ann Bailey, at All Saints, Ockham,

44 Kneeler commemorating the Golden Jubilee of the Diocese of Guildford. Designed by Jane Black for All Saints, Ockham.

Surrey. For the prayer desk in front of the bishop's chair at St Kieran Episcopal Church, Campbeltown, Argyllshire, Ursula Allen based a mitre and crook design on the coat-of-arms of the Bishop of Argyll and the Isles.

At Hingham, a small town of 2,000 people in mid-Norfolk, many of the 300 kneelers were inspired by heraldic devices in the Church of St Andrew, notably the six shields at the base of the Morley tomb in the chancel. (Pevsner considers this, built of red stone, to be one of the most impressive fifteenth-century wall monuments in the country.)

The Priory Church of St Lawrence, Snaith, in Humberside, was formerly called after the ancient Christian settlement of St Osyth's. The church commands the old town which stands on the River Aire at a point where travellers from Lincoln crossed on their way to York. That is why, as well as the diocesan arms of Sheffield, there are kneelers that carry the arms of Lincoln and York.

'The best things are in the Choir,' a priest told us as we entered Ripon Cathedral in Yorkshire. He was speaking of the intricately carved misericords, and of the east window tracery; but, for the purpose of our book, the kneelers were also the best. Worked throughout in tent stitch, they

45   The naval crown, designed by Joan Bedale from a woodcarving in the chapel of the Queen's Royal Surrey Regiment in Guildford Cathedral, for the church of St Lawrence, Effingham.

have lime green backgrounds and narrow jade green borders. There are three designs: the keys of St Peter (patron saint, with St Wilfrid); three starfish (for St Wilfrid, by tradition a fisherman); and seven lozenges or diamond shapes, worked in a mixture of turquoise and pale blue. The lozenges represent both the seven hills of Rome – which Wilfrid visited to appeal against the division of the See of York – and his fishing net. Thus, at Ripon, we find a departure from the more familiar saintly symbols.

One of the most easily recognizable of these, St Katharine of Alexandria's wheel, recalls the patron saint of a little Norman church at Knockholt, in Kent. More elaborate, and involving the use of lettering as well as symbolism, is the series at St Andrew, Sevenhampton, in the Cotswolds. Designed and organized by a former vicar, the late Canon F. H. Charles, 21 New Testament and 27 Early English saints adorn the chancel. Hugh has his tame swan and John a stately eagle; fish swim across Andrew's diagonal cross; while Gabriel's kneeler reminds us that he brought the tidings to Mary. Background details and colour

shading add to the charms of these kneelers carried out in cross, rice, and (to join the corners) long leg cross stitch. The simplicity of the stitches and the coarse canvas (seven stitches to the inch) suit the plain interior. In this small community it was found that anybody who was willing could make a successful kneeler. One embroiderer chose to do St Ethelburga because her name is Ethel! Canon Charles's clear charts helped enormously.

St Botolph, Boston, in Lincolnshire, is usually known, because it has a 288 foot tower rather than a spire, as Boston Stump. Built on the edge of the tidal river Witham, the church has been flooded many times, and when the old kneelers were damaged by water in January 1978, this merely spurred on the replacement scheme just begun. The idea was to celebrate the twelve apostles; and Ronald Sims, the church architect, made sure that these kneelers had room for both the apostles' emblems and their names. Two other designs, the Boston coat-of-arms and an outline of the church itself, completed the series. In all, 324 kneelers, made in a variety of colour schemes, were dedicated in April, 1979.

Often the simplest ideas are the most surprising. At Stock, near Ingatestone in Essex, the designs are based on a shadow 'S', for the

46   The arms of the State of Maryland, commemorating the visit of Mr and Mrs Harpole of Baltimore to the village of Harpole in Northamptonshire.

patronal All Saints, and for Stock. At St Martin, East Horsley, Surrey, in a plan for the recently built extension, the kneelers have blue backgrounds to go with the upholstery of the chairs, and each features a light blue triangle which represents St Martin's cloak. Jean Huband, the Rector's wife, has organized the scheme; Hanni Bailey designed the kneelers.

At Carston, a small village five miles from Bath, a group of embroiderers aged between nine and ninety provided All Saints Church with kneelers designed by Mrs C. J. Taylor, a relation of a parishioner. On gold backgrounds, these depict lives of the saints worked in cross and rice stitches in mixed colours. They were made in the early Sixties, and are wearing well.

Not unnaturally, many designs are related to the church's patron saint. In the fine St Mary Magdalene, Taunton, every kneeler has its central monogram of linked 'M's; those in the small church of St Lawrence-in-the-Square, Winchester, varied in treatment and many, by the Revd Peter Gallup, have rust-coloured backgrounds. On the sides of all of them St Lawrence's gridiron is worked. His courage is also celebrated among Christian symbols on two short altar kneelers, a united effort, in the side chapel at St Lawrence, Snaith.

Ursula Allen, who began the project on her own at St Kieran, Campbeltown, received a kneeler decorated with a Welsh dragon flag. This startled her; the church, after all, was in Scotland. She discovered that the embroiderer had made the design in memory of her Welsh husband. Mrs Allen decided that they should add kneelers for St Andrew, St George and St Patrick; and because the row in which they were placed needed one more, she used a design that took in the thistle, rose, daffodil, and shamrock.

When, in 1650, Lady Anne Clifford, mistress of so many great mansions and castles, was widowed for the second time, she decided to do something for other widows. Appleby was one of her four northern castles. It was here, 1651–3, in what was the county town of Westmorland (but is now in Cumbria) that she built almshouses known as the Hospital of St Anne, for twelve 'Sisters', old and infirm women of the neighbourhood, and a senior one known as the Mother. The houses exist to this day round a central courtyard on the east side of Boroughgate; recently their chapel was furnished with kneelers which bear Lady Anne's coat-of-arms.

47   The Agincourt Rose, designed by Louisa Pesel for Winchester Cathedral.

His keys are almost certain to be found somewhere on kneelers in churches dedicated to St Peter. They are on every kneeler in Exeter Cathedral; and at St Peter, Pimperne, Blandford Forum, Dorset, they were an essential part of the first 60 kneelers made there. Because the parish is connected with Henry VII and Henry VIII, the Tudor rose and portcullis were worked into the next series.

Another rose appears, centrally, on one of Louisa Pesel's designs in Winchester Cathedral. It is the Agincourt, or Lancastrian, Rose, which has a local significance. As a reward for their prowess at the Battle of Agincourt, Henry V awarded the Rose to volunteers from Southamptonshire (which we know as Hampshire). The Rose is now incorporated in the Arms of the City of Southampton and has been worn by the Hampshire Regiment for over a hundred years.

In St Paul's Chapel, church house of the Diocese of Southern Ohio in Cincinnati, parishioners throughout the diocese worked kneelers to honour the patron saints of their churches. On the altar kneelers, designed by the Revd John Heale, then curate-in-charge of St Michael and All Angels, Little Horsted, Uckfield, Sussex, St

Michael fights the dragon in the centre, and on each side angels kneel. Another Sussex church, at Iford, near Lewes, is faithful to Nicholas, its patron saint.

Many churches called after All Saints match their kneelers to their dedication. So All Saints, East Winch, Norfolk, has a series in reds and blues: St Ambrose (mitre); St Nicholas (dove); St Hugh (swan); St Peter (keys); St Mary the Virgin (Sacred Heart); and others. (See also *Wedding kneelers*.)

Logos could be described as the heraldry of the present and future. Instead of St Peter's keys or St Hugh's swan, some kneeler schemes employ logos as their linking symbols. At St Mary the Virgin, Wimbledon, London, every kneeler must bear its special 'W' logo. (See also *Local history* and *Personal*.)

At St Edmund, Mansfield Woodhouse, Nottinghamshire, they obtained from Jackson's Rugcraft a design for their patron saint. This St Edmund's kneeler is placed by the altar for the use of the clergy and church officials.

Among the coats-of-arms in St Sepulchre-without-Newgate in London, one kneeler is worked with that of the Worshipful Company of Broderers (who honoured Louisa Pesel), and, suitably, because this church is renowned for its

OMNIA DESUPER

48 The arms of the Broderers Company, in the Church of the Holy Sepulchre-without-Newgate, in the City of London.

49 The arms of the Royal Academy of Music, in the Church of the Holy Sepulchre-without-Newgate.

PRESERVE HARMONY

50   Personal kneeler for the Dean of Lincoln, which depicts his family coat-of-arms, that of Saye and Sele. The seals are worked in velvet stitch.

musical associations, there is one with the arms of the Royal Academy of Music. (See also *Hands across the sea* and *Words and music*.)

Seals, worked in velvet stitch, are part of the Dean's coat-of-arms on his kneeler in Lincoln Cathedral.

Of the many birds in heraldry, the one most commonly seen is the eagle, often given two heads facing in opposite directions. Worked in tent, long leg and wheatsheaf, one appears, with variations of stitches but in the same colours, at St Peter and St Paul, Kirton, near Boston, Lincolnshire. The shading of the wings must have been difficult, but these are in the main kneelers expertly managed, with backgrounds of contrasting greens.

St Peter's Anglican Church at Brockville, Ontario, has a chapel dedicated to St Alban. This goes back to the time when St Alban's School was in Brockville, and the kneeler here has St Alban's Roman shield, sword and mace, together with his cross. Because he was the first English martyr – a Roman soldier converted to Christianity while he was on military service – there are also oak leaves (for England) and maple leaves (for Canada).

In the local tradition

Through the arch of what has been described as 'a cottage with the ground floor removed' (*c.*1600), you reach the church of St Peter and St Paul at Long Compton in Warwickshire. Begun in the thirteenth century, the north arcade and aisle were added in the fourteenth. This is sheep country; wool has been important to the lives of its inhabitants ever since the Middle Ages. During the sixteenth century William Sheldon, a neighbouring landlord, sent one Richard Hicks to the Netherlands to learn the craft of weaving; on his return, Hicks set up looms at Barcheston for the manufacture of 'arras, moccadoes, carolles, plonketts, grosgraynes, says and sarges'. They prospered, and examples of Barcheston tapestry hang in the Bodleian Library in Oxford and in the Victoria & Albert Museum. As late as the mid eighteenth century Horace Walpole bought some fine pieces for £30, which he considered 'very cheap indeed'.

So now, although it is embroidered rather than woven, we cannot be surprised to find a carpet in the chancel at Long Compton. It is as if the local needlewomen had followed a local tradition. Under Myra Waterson's guidance they began in the late 1950s, stitching birds of the air and flowers of the field inspired by Queen

Mary's carpet which, worked in *gros point*, had gone on a dollar-raising tour of the States and Canada. (To Queen Mary's delight, it was bought for £35,000 by the Imperial Daughters of the Empire. 'This is my gift towards the National Debt!!' she wrote in her diary.) It is now in the National Museum in Ottawa.

At Long Compton, members of the Churchwomen's Guild worked sections (one bird, or one flower) separately; Mrs Waterson stitched them together. They used rug canvas and Turkey rug wool, which meant that though the stitches (cross) are larger then most, the finished effect is not unpleasing. Each needlewoman received a pack of short lengths of wool, carefully measured. As rug wool is expensive, Mrs Waterson decided that she could not spare them at one time as much as an ounce of each colour (in all, they incorporated 21). At the beginning they held vicarage coffee mornings to make money for the materials, which were bought in Stratford-upon-Avon. The idea of the carpet soon caught on, 'like a disease'. When complete, it gave colour and lightness where the church had been dull and dark, so the Vicar, the Revd E.

J. Rainsberry, told us. The border motifs derived from the stained glass windows.

Because mice had attacked the old kneelers, Mrs Waterson and her team went on to make new ones of the same materials as the carpet. Against blue backgrounds, crosses of various shapes, worked in yellow and gold, formed the centrepieces. Only the tops of the 70 kneelers were embroidered; the sides and bases are of green fabric-backed vinyl, and the filling was done professionally by a London firm.

The Long Compton 'disease' did not end with the chancel carpet and kneelers. They also made plain blue runners with narrow gold borders for the pews, and they inspired other schemes in neighbouring churches. Thus, at Whichford, the de Mohun coat-of-arms is remembered by an engrailed cross on the kneelers; and for those in private chapels at Castle Ashby and Compton Wynyates, seats of the Northampton family, Myra Waterson gave her advice.

Worstead in Norfolk is also the name of the cloth which was first woven there. More recently, inside the church of St Mary, they spun wool and used the cloth on kneelers. Did the wool come from the sheep in the churchyard? If so, it would be a perfect example of a well-rounded tale.

51   The holly and the ivy, from All Saints, Harpole, Northamptonshire.

In memoriam

In his *Companion Guide to London* David Piper describes the collection of 800 kneelers at St Clement Danes in the Strand as 'a dazzle of brilliant little hassocks'. Like Chelsea Old Church, St Clement Danes was badly damaged during the Second World War. In 1958 the restored building was made the Central Church of the Royal Air Force, so it is hardly surprising to discover a great deal of Air Force blue on the kneelers, as well as many other blues. (It is also the patron saint's colour.) There are many 'In memory of . . .' designs with initials, also some made and given as thank-offerings for the safe return of airmen; but this is only part of a scheme organized by Nancy Kimmins, who also designed many of the kneelers and advised embroiderers from all over the world. (See also *Rich and rare*.)

In some churches, the names or initials of incumbents are perpetuated on kneelers: at Holy Trinity, Bosham, West Sussex, the initials go back to the thirteenth century. (See also *Local history*.)

At St Andrew, Holt, in north Norfolk, kneelers in memory of airmen (from the local RAF station) have their initials and dates on one side and the initials of the embroiderer on the other. This is also the method at St Nicholas, Blakeney, on the Norfolk coast. At St Andrew, Enfield, in Middlesex, dates and initials are worked in gold; and among a number of memorial kneelers at St Edmund, Mansfield Woodhouse, Nottinghamshire, those for men killed in action have the names of their regiments, or, on one kneeler recently made, that of HMS *Antelope*. St John the Baptist, Boldre, tucked away in the New Forest, has been turned into a memorial for men lost at sea in HMS *Hood*: the kneelers there, all worked in *petit point*, are evocative. Service crests are among the designs at St George, Thriplow, Cambridgeshire.

At St Edward, Shaugh Prior, South Devon, in memoriam kneelers have names and dates on the long sides, and upon the short ones crosses and the Scouting 'Gone home' sign. (See also *Two by two*.)

In memory of Eileen Lucy Wade, who had lived for many years in Upper Dean, Bedfordshire, her son Christopher and his wife Diana offered to provide materials to cover the old kneelers in All Hallows Church. The idea was to associate each one with a local inhabitant known

to Mrs Wade, so this could be described as a double memorial programme. A bell and spade are worked into the sexton's kneeler, and a border of postage stamps for his wife, the postmistress; for the parish clerk, pen and inkpot; for the church caretaker, candlesticks; for the organist, the organ and a phrase of music; for the blacksmith, an anvil and horseshoe. Relations were asked to make their own designs, if possible; Diana Wade drew them on graph paper. The scheme took off; people stayed up half the night working at the kneelers, though at first they had protested that they did not know how to do the cross stitch used throughout. But they could not give up; they were so pleased to have their relations commemorated in this way. Names and dates were worked here on the kneeler sides. (See also *The church mouse* and *Local history*.)

The Irish connection

Sixteen kneelers in St Patrick's Chapel, Glastonbury Abbey, Somerset, reflect a close connection with the Celtic world and with Ireland in particular. Relics at Glastonbury have been claimed as St Patrick's – a claim which cannot be contradicted or substantiated, since no one knows where he was buried.

All the designs originate in early Irish art; they are taken from objects made of bronze, silver, and precious stones. Others come from illuminated manuscripts: the ninth-century Book of Kells, and St John's Gospel in the seventh-century Book of Durrow, both at Trinity College, Dublin. The objects which suggested the designs are now museum pieces, chiefly in the National Museum of Ireland. Miraculously, they have survived over the centuries. The Book of Durrow, named from the monastery where it was compiled, escaped disaster even after one of its owners, a farmer, dipped it in his cows' pond to protect the animals from disease. The Tara Brooch, made in eighth-century Ireland of gilded bronze, and decorated richly with gold filigree, amber, enamel, and amethyst, seems to have been stolen by a Viking raider who took it home. With other Scandinavian treasures it was brought back in a box which was found in County Meath, near the mouth of the Boyne and not far from Tara, the ancient capital; hence its name. A boy, digging in a potato field a hundred

52 The crowing cockerels of St Clement Danes,
worked in rice, long leg, cushion, gobelin and fern
stitches. Designed by Nancy Kimmins.

53   The Eagle of St John, a design taken from the Book of Kells, at St Margaret's, Laceby, near Grimsby.

years ago, discovered a silver chalice engraved with the names of the Apostles. And one of the most engaging kneeler designs, that of a dog with his tail in his mouth to symbolize 'completeness', is based upon a brooch; it appears on Irish stamps, as well as on one of the kneelers in St Patrick's Chapel.

There are 12 kneelers for the congregation, one for the priest at the altar, and a set of three at the altar steps. Worked in tent stitch during 1978/9 by embroiderers of Moorlinch, the col-our scheme is green for the background, with shades of gold and brown.

Taken from the Book of Kells, a magnificent eagle dominates a kneeler in a variety of stitches at St Margaret, Laceby, in Lincolnshire, as part of a scheme organized by Ingrid Read.

Kneeler fever

How did kneeler fever spread to America? There are rumours of a high-ranking clergyman visiting Britain, seeing kneelers, and returning home determined: 'We must have some here.' During the fifties Mrs Harold Talbott, wife of the secretary of the US Air Force, organized a group of women in Washington, DC, to start needlepointing for the National Cathedral, Mount St Alban. In 1954 they formed a committee for the care of canvas work in the Cathedral. About this time four sisters called Tebbet, from Connecticut, designed a carpet to lead up five steps to the High Altar; and 23 women from the Diocese of Pittsburgh made it. The two kneelers at the High Altar complement the Tebbet carpet, with a design for the Cathedral's two saints, Peter and Paul. Other kneelers have pentecostal emblems, and those along 30 feet of the communion rail are decorated with symbols of the Eucharist and butterflies for the Resurrection.

In St John's Chapel portraits of famous men are worked in tent stitch on bright red grounds. In gratitude for American aid during the Second World War, British women, including the Queen Mother herself, made kneelers for the War Memorial Chapel; and, in St Joseph of Arimathea's Chapel in the crypt, altar kneelers now match the mural.

So many American needlepointers assure us that the National Cathedral kneelers are show pieces. Their beginnings, undoubtedly, started a remarkable trend in all parts of the country. They take kneeler making seriously; for example, at Grace Episcopal Church, Winfield, Kansas, they spent a year studying and a year 'actually doing'. At another American church they studied slides of kneelers from the National Cathedral. For 26 kneelers (and other sanctuary needlepoint) at St John the Baptist Episcopal Church, Seattle, in the State of Washington, Guild members devoted over a year to planning and designing before stitching began.

Several of our North American correspondents have told us where to look for special kneelers in the United Kingdom. They have recommended those at Mawnan Smith, always considered to have some of the best in Cornwall; and Constance Vulliamy of Parkville, Missouri, describes an experience she had while in England in 1985:

The beautiful church in Zennor, Cornwall, has the most exquisite needlepoint kneelers imaginable throughout the entire church. They were begun in 1977 to celebrate the centenary of Truro Diocese and the Queen's Silver Jubilee ... We were fortunate enough to be there on Saturday afternoon, 11 May, when we found the entire (and I do mean entire)

church filled with garden flowers and the fragrance was beyond telling. Two ladies were still adding more flowers, and we were told that the next day was their saint's feast day and also the annual parade of the West Cornwall Burma Star Association (the Vicar is their Chaplain).

It was something we'll not forget.

Many of the kneelers at the church of St Senara, Zennor, far down in West Cornwall, derive from kits, but there is also some original work. One in particular delights everybody who visits the church. Although, according to John Betjeman, St Senara was 'scraped inside of its texture in 1890', not quite everything old went; a mermaid carved into a fifteenth-century bench-end remains as part of a seat in the sanctuary. She looks into a mirror that she holds with one hand while combing her long tresses with the other. It is not surprising that she is there, for (as Geoffrey Grigson has said) mermaids, born as the singing sirens of Greek myth, are familiar in church carvings and paintings. They warn the Christian of snares which await him during 'his voyage through the wickedness of the world'. The mermaid of Zennor has also found a place on a kneeler.

Mary P. Olsen, of South Brooksville, Maine, author of a handbook on kneelers, *For the Greater Glory*, took photographs of cathedrals and parish churches in England as the basis of a slide-show that is now hired out to organizations. Besides being in charge of one programme in Keene, New Hampshire, which produced 438 pieces of needlepoint, she has been consultant to 31 other churches.

Obviously, interest is immense, and the standard of work is high. American visitors to Britain are often astonished to find kneelers in all parts of the church, however, because their own are usually confined to the altar rail and to the sanctuary. As one woman said: 'To fill the nave would be a very long job.'

Local history

Probably the most satisfying subject for a kneeler project – at least, for the inhabitants – is something essentially local, something that happened at this church, or in this village, a building or a feature of the landscape. Every kneeler project in the country could include a series of crosses, or texts, or bars of music, or emblems or

54 Falling priest, from St Mary-at-Latton, Harlow (photograph by Bob Gibson).

symbols, but no church other than St Mary-at-Latton, Harlow, Essex, could record the astonishing fact that in 1234 a chaplain called Ernoldus fell to his death from the Norman tower. Here, on one of the sixteen sanctuary kneelers, he plunges head first past a surprised seagull. This dramatic event, translated into embroidery, called for a variety of stitches: jacquard for the sky; cashmere for the brick tower; rhodes, cushion, alternating cross, and, for the chaplain's face, *petit point*. According to the kneelers, Latton people were inclined to take matters into their own hands; in 1641 bellringers who disapproved of the new altar rails simply burnt them.

In 1964 someone set fire to the church; the tower showed signs of crumbling, so the build-ing was fully restored in 1972. There are probably other kneelers which feature bleak modern architecture such as tower blocks, but none is more appropriate than one at Latton representing Harlow New Town, which swallowed up rural Latton but left its 900-year-old church. (See also *Peal of bells*.)

We have found many other examples of local subjects. In St John the Baptist, Findon, near Worthing, a forge appears on one of the 200 kneelers. The blacksmith is still active in this neighbourhood, famous for its racing stables. When we asked the vicar, Canon E. R. Gillies, the way to the home of the organizer, Alice Wright, he told us to go past the post office – and there it was, to guide us, on a kneeler. In a church containing fragments of twelfth-century wall paintings, it is startling to find modern telephone boxes on a kneeler. (See also *Natural history* and *Wedding kneelers*.)

In the little Victorian church of Christ Church, Shamley Green, Surrey, Peggy Scott, a former rector's wife, inaugurated a scheme for the ten altar kneelers: each embroiderer produced a portrait of her own house and its surroundings. Gold and cyclamen predominate among the colours and a great many different stitches lend perspective.

Among the 170 kneelers at St Mary the Virgin, Wimbledon, several local scenes are worked on blue backgrounds with yellow borders, since blue and yellow are the Virgin's colours. There are ponies on the Common, the lawn-tennis championships (with changing fashions from long skirts to shorts), and even foxes in a suburban garden. (See also *Personal*.)

Local landmarks stand out on kneelers at St Mary Magdalene, Mulbarton, which has the largest green in Norfolk; here it is, triangular-shaped, complete with duck and lily pond. For the water long leg cross stitch was used, turning the canvas for each row; the ripples were achieved by working in two strands of green wool and one of blue. Another effective local subject was a six-storey smock mill, demolished in 1849. To indicate the structure of the sails, upright cross stitch and plait stitch were worked diagonally. On another of the nine designs a simple repeating pattern was formed from the shape of gables found on buildings in the village. (See also *Stained glass*.)

For its size – a population of 600 – Middleham, North Yorkshire, is fortunate in its tumultuous medieval history from which a designer can learn a great deal. The Castle, with its immense Norman keep, is known as the Windsor of the North. The young Duke of Gloucester (later Richard III) lived there when it was Warwick the Kingmaker's headquarters, and later he remained with his wife Anne Neville, whose family owned the Castle. Kneelers in the parish church reflect local history: the white rose of York, Richard's white boar, the Castle itself.

Margaret Nixon based her earliest designs on variations of the cross, but as her needlewomen became more proficient they were able to follow historical designs. Not all the kneelers have been made locally; in these days Middleham is a tourist place, and not only because of the Wars of the Roses. This is Herriot country; perhaps soon we may expect the best-selling vet to be featured on a kneeler. Many visitors have offered to make kneelers – not yet of Herriot, so far as we know – and one is being made in America.

One of the most original ideas in design came to Canon R. G. Chaffey-Moore, former rector of the Victorian Gothic church of St Mary, Compton Abbas, in Dorset. When his church was 100 years old, in 1968, parishioners decided to complete the furnishing of the side aisle by making a sanctuary carpet with kneelers to match. He had been saddened to see so many hedges in the surrounding countryside removed, and so it was decided to record the old field names on the kneelers. After a great deal of research, names such as Whitsun Acre and Monks Mead were identified on maps and in records. Older inhabitants could point to their whereabouts, and the kneelers were made with green backgrounds, the field names in yellow and the borders in blue and yellow. In one corner, in their natural colours, each kneeler has a bunch of flowers which might have grown there. Thus we find a fragment of lost history embroidered in tent stitch and long leg cross stitch, and worked in thrums from the Wilton carpet factory.

Okewood Church (originally 'Chappell') goes back to 1220, so there is much history to incorporate on its kneelers. In the fifteenth century a miracle is said to have saved a man attacked by a boar; in the sixteenth century the Crown seized the land and dissolved the Chappell, so parishioners' tears at its loss form the design; petitions failed until Elizabeth I restored its 'Honest Pryeste'. John Evelyn, the diarist, who lived at nearby Wotton, and his descendants, patrons of Okewood, are also remembered. Designs are by Jennifer Dyer.

St Erth, near St Ives, has been described as 'one of the unforgettable villages in Cornwall'. It is also known for the British Rail announcement on Paddington-to-Penzance trains, 'Change at St Erth for St Ives.' It lies on the now silted-up Hayle River which is crossed by a four-arched Elizabethan bridge. In the little church of St Ercus, one of the remoter saints, the Lady Chapel is called after the great house of Trewinnard, formerly the seat of the Lords Mohun and Arundel. The old coach road used to run over the bridge and one of the earliest coaches, reasonably enough the Trewinnard, now stands in state at the County Museum in Truro. Both the bridge and the coach are commemorated on kneelers. Mary Wells, wife of the vicar at the time they furnished the Trewinnard Chapel, designed them. (See also *Look about you*.)

55   The Customs House, Lancaster, for the church of St George's in the Marsh, Lancaster.

A river runs through the history of Snaith in Humberside, at the other end of the country. It is the River Aire, and they have put the old toll-bridge on a kneeler at the Priory Church of St Lawrence. This is especially apt because in old times travellers from Lincoln crossed the river here and found food and shelter before setting forth to York. Other local references on kneelers: cooling towers; pithead machinery; a miner's lamp.

'Sweet Thames, run softly . . .', wrote Spenser. Appropriately, the river does run softly, in a wavy line in three shades of blue, through or round every kneeler in the imaginatively conceived set at St Nicholas, Thames Ditton. Appropriately, because the church stands on the Surrey bank of the Thames. (See also *Look about you*, *Personal*, and *Sacred and secular*.)

Holy Cross, at Ramsbury in Wiltshire, is a much restored Saxon foundation, and the tale of its kneelers is a classic progress from simplicity to elaboration. Under Marian Davies, the vicar's wife, parishioners began with plain kneelers for a side-chapel, working on coarse canvas in thrums from the Wilton carpet factory near Salisbury. They then moved on to the main part of the church, and, presently, many crosses (for the church's dedication) appeared on a set of 250 kneelers. By then they were growing in skill and could tackle something more detailed on finer canvas and with finer wool. Some of the altar kneeler designs have two meanings: the fish, a Christian symbol, is also a trout leaping in the River Kennet which runs through the village; while the bread and grapes are there not only for the Eucharist, but also because of an ancient corn mill and vineyard in the neighbourhood. Finally, a raven has its own panel because the place was once called Ravensbury, and a mitre celebrates the fact that in 902 Ramsbury was a Saxon bishopric.

The village of Little Horsted, Uckfield, East Sussex, has 60 houses, and each has its individual kneeler in the church of St Michael and All Angels. The name of the house appears on the front, and on the top an appropriate picture. One local farm has a cow, another a horse; a cottage has a couple of ducks, another a dog; there are flowers that grow in the gardens, and Acorn Cottage, obviously, is decorated with an oak branch. The kneeler for Horsted Place, former home of Lord and Lady Rupert Nevill, depicts wild arum lilies (or 'lords and ladies'), complete with spotted leaves and heads of scarlet berries. The local undertaker's kneeler has a cross of coffins. A quirky sense of humour seems to have been at work.

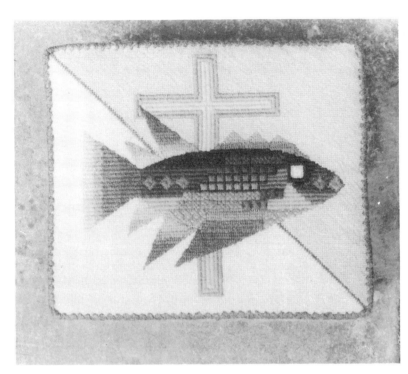

56 Fish embroidered in rice, gobelin, rumanian, cushion, eyelet, half rhodes, and tent stitch, for the church of St Margaret, Laceby, Lincolnshire.

57 Lord Buckingham's jerkin, on a kneeler made by Dame Joan Sutherland for All Saints, Brightlingsea, in Essex. This commemorates his gift of a jerkin to Lord D'Arcy of St Osyth in 1600, with a request to stop the men of St Osyth coming up the river to steal the Brightlingsea oysters.

The general idea came from the Revd John Heale, curate in charge when parishioners started to make kneelers. He and Isolde Wigram designed them; Miss Wigram painted the designs directly on to the canvas. Miss E. Kennedy also played an important part in the scheme. The interpretation varied according to the inclination and talent of the embroiderer. Backgrounds are either blue or red; borders are gold; tent stitch is used throughout, ten stitches to the inch on double canvas. When the Bishop of Lewes blessed the kneelers, he told the packed congregation: 'It is good that every family has its own kneeler. Do come sometimes and kneel on it and say your prayers.'

A map of the village, designed by John Heale, hangs in the church. Every house (and so every kneeler) is marked. John Heale died before the map was finished, so it was completed by Isolde Wigram.

Lord Buckingham's jerkin – one of the designs at All Saints, Brightlingsea, Essex – goes back to 1600, when his Lordship, Warden of the Cinque Ports, sent his jerkin to Lord D'Arcy of St Osyth, asking him to stop the men of St Osyth from coming up the river and stealing the Brightlingsea oysters. Brightlingsea, formerly a 'limb' of the Cinque Ports, is very proud of its connections.

All Saints is a hilltop church overlooking the Colne estuary; it is said that the splendid tower can be seen 12 miles out at sea. Preserved in the church they keep a lamp which, during bad weather 150 years ago, the vicar used to light and hang in the tower to guide the fishing boats home. This lamp is on the kneelers, and so is the shield, with three lions and boats, used by the mayor and mayoress when they visit the church. Because the area is involved in the fishing industry, and seafaring in general, the kneelers record boats of all sorts: trawlers, fishing boats, barges, sailing boats, tankers, and the lifeboat. In about 653 a little ship brought St Cedd, bishop of the East Saxons, as a missionary from Lindisfarne to Bradwell-on-Sea, some distance from which he built a chapel. Every year parishioners make a pilgrimage – by boat, of course – from Brightlingsea, across the estuary to the barn-like chapel, St Peter's-on-the-Wall, remote and ancient, between the sea and the salt-marshes.

Fish invariably look well in canvas work. There is a charming one at Brightlingsea, drawn by the children of St James's Church School, as

58   The lamp which was hung on the church tower of All Saints, Brightlingsea, to guide the fishermen safely home. Designed by L. B. Simeon.

59 The ship in which St Cedd sailed from Lindisfarne to Bradwell, where he founded a chapel. Designed by L. B. Simeon.

60 Designed by the children of St James's Church School in Brightlingsea, to commemorate the school's existence, just before it was closed.

a memento of the school which has now closed. More local history!

In All Hallows, Upper Dean, Bedfordshire, they have remembered 'local worthies' (as they used to be called): the squire, the lay rector who paid for re-roofing the chancel, and Professor Albert Richardson, architect to York Minster, who was responsible for repairs and conservation at Upper Dean during the 1920s. There is a kneeler with the crossed keys of the Knights Hospitallers, who held the church from the twelfth century to the Reformation, and one from the brass of Thomas Parker, a fifteenth-century vicar. A Book of Isaiah stands for Francis Bellingham (born at Upper Dean), who translated it for the King James Bible. The church, the spire, the old clock and the weather-vane all have kneelers. Many in the 117 village households knew little of their church history before the project began in 1974; it aroused curiosity and caused, to the general delight, the discovery of inter-family relationships.

Local historians of the future will perhaps not think of kneelers as archives; but they could do worse. The grey stone school building of standard architecture, is disappearing in the smaller communities (where, incidentally, we find some of the best kneelers). This has happened at Lelant, in the west of Cornwall, where the old school is now a dwelling house. In the church of St Uny it has been recorded, with children in its playground, on a kneeler.

Other Cornish schemes have included such features of the local landscape as the tin mine, now fast crumbling into disuse, and the light-house, which still remains but may be replaced one day by automation. One thing is certain: two features of the Cornish holiday – the golf course and the bucket and spade – are here to stay, and they have been given kneelers of their own.

It would be exciting if it could be proved that the Bosham Ecclesia of the Bayeux Tapestry (which is not a tapestry, but a strip of embroidered linen) was truly the church of Holy Trinity, Bosham, in West Sussex, or at least one on the site. Scholars have argued against it, maintaining that, because two churches are recorded at Bosham in the Domesday Book, it is likely that Harold would have gone to the other, which was attached to his manor. All the same, it is human and natural that at this church where fragments of the Anglo-Saxon building remain, embroideries in the form of altar frontal and kneelers should perpetuate the association with

Canute (whose daughter is buried in the church) and Harold, who is given a kneeler with a crown and the date 1064, as well as with the Tapestry itself.

The Bosham kneelers, all different, are only 3.5 centimetres ($1\frac{2}{5}$ in.) deep; they rest upon the older leather ones. On the edges of the blue backgrounds there are chain-link borders in gold. As might be expected in this yachting centre, many designs are connected with the sea: gulls, shells, galleons, and sailing ships. (See also *In memoriam*.)

Some of the most lively pictorial designs we have seen are those at St Lawrence, Effingham, Surrey. Organized and designed by Joan Bedale and Jessica Page, the scheme began in 1966 with a tremendous spurt of energy. Over 70 workers completed 130 kneelers in two years. The group of Canterbury pilgrims on their steeds seem capable of trotting out of the canvas. There are others with local historical connections: the Churchill oak, the Wallis oak made to commemorate Sir Barnes Wallis's eightieth birthday, and the stylized roe deer in Effingham Forest (real ones still venture into the village).

To celebrate the 150th anniversary of St Peter's Anglican Church at Brockville in Ontario, their Altar Guild made seven altar kneelers which, uniquely, reflect Brockville's geographical situation. It is in the middle of the Thousand Islands along the St Lawrence River; so the central panels are diversely island-shaped, and each island has three symbols. Some are the familiar Christian symbols, beautifully designed by Marjorie Winslow, an artist known across Canada: the fish, dove, lamb, ship, anchor, crown of thorns, Chi Rho, grapes (wine), and wheat (bread). Some are local, such as mallards and Canada geese: and two represent St Peter: his upside-down cross, and the cock (crowing thrice). Vera Griffith, a needlepoint teacher from Kingston, gave advice and support throughout the scheme.

Gillian Anstis, who had never done any needlepointing before, describes the experience:

It has been a great satisfaction to be working on something for St Peter's Church; it has made me feel closer to the church, and I have enjoyed getting to know more people in the congregation and working with them . . . I have gained more than I have given.

She 'gave' the beehive on one of the altar kneelers (a design from the coat-of-arms of the city of Brockville). There were times, she admits to us, when it became a bit wearisome, but her

61 The Canterbury Pilgrims, designed by Joan
Bedale for St Lawrence, Effingham, Surrey.

62 Effingham Forest, designed by Joan Bedale
for St Lawrence, Effingham, Surrey.

63 Holy Trinity, Wetheral, Carlisle. Mason's mark on an archway in the church. Gold ground in plaited gobelin stitch. The border shapes are taken from the viaduct which crosses the valley, and are in two shades which match the red sandstone of which the church is built.

husband came to the rescue, reading aloud a book on Dickens which they both enjoyed, and she found, too, a pet name for each of the three bees on her kneeler.

I was, to put it mildly [she says], slightly apprehensive. However, I set to work, counted holes, counted stitches, learned quickly how to be ambidextrous, and slowly (*very* slowly), my first picture evolved. A few impressions from my first efforts – the monotony; the counting and marking off of the stitches on the chart; finding a comfortable position in which to work; the heat of the summer evenings; the callouses on my thumbs. But I'm sure they will beautify St Peter's for many years to come and I'm thrilled to have had a small part in the making of them.

(See also *Heraldry* and *Natural history*.)

Colour is an important part of the kneeler scheme in the Howard Chapel which is now part of Wetheral Parish Church, Cumbria. The background is the red of the local sandstone from which the church is built. The designers looked about them both inside and outside. Thus, there are kneelers worked in Hungarian, encroaching gobelin, Parisian, tent and florentine stitches, on which there appears a mason's mark – the letter M with a cross bar on the left – taken from one upon a pillar; the rose of the Howard family; and the Cross with the ring on the wrought iron screen. (The ring symbolizes eternity.)

For their kneelers at St Nicholas, Salthouse, Norfolk, Dorothy Sowter told us:

We have considered very carefully the character of our church; its environment, and the local interests in this small coastal village. When designing I believe strongly in that approach and feel that what is suitable in a city church could look out of place elsewhere. Colour, too, has its importance. Designs for the chancel have been in wine colours and to tone with the altar cloth; in the nave soft vegetable greens have been the unifying colours with the addition of one other from the general scheme if needed. These seemed to fit in with the environment and also the size of the church. Brightly coloured coarsely embroidered kneelers would have broken up the general scheme in this huge, lofty, beautiful church.

There is much here for the newcomer to kneeler

64 The ancient tiles in the floor of Winchester Cathedral.

65 Kneeler inspired by the tiles shown in fig. 64.

projects to heed. As Dorothy Sowter believes, colour is all-important. Wisely, Dr Paradise and Mrs Lidington, organizers at St Nicholas, Cranleigh, Surrey, sought at the beginning professional advice on the choice of colours.

At St Ercus, St Erth, in Cornwall, they have kneelers copied from bench-end carvings; and at another church in west Cornwall, St Senara, Zennor, there is one from a rather special bench-end. (See also *Kneeler fever.*) The entire scheme at St Mary, Great Bealings, Suffolk, comes from 12 poppy heads carved with crests of former local Lords of the Manor, two churchwardens, and the Rector, Canon Edward Moor, who was responsible for the careful restoration of the church in mid-Victorian times.

66 The Cheke Brass, from St Nicholas's Church, Thames Ditton. The wavy border represents the River Thames (photograph by Brian Moore).

Look about you

Those pioneers, Louisa Pesel and Sybil Blunt, founders of the Winchester Cathedral Broderers, certainly looked about them when they chose the colours for their kneelers and stall cushions. They simply looked upward at the bosses in the Cathedral roof – and there was a ready-made colour scheme. When the Second World War dispersed many of her workers, Miss Pesel had to fall back on the girls from Atherley School, Southampton, who were evacuated to Winchester. For the kneelers they made in the Lady Chapel she looked at the floor of the Retro-Choir and based her designs on the ancient tiles. (See also page 13.)

At St Nicholas, Thames Ditton, their first kneeler reproduced the metal decoration on the font cover. Later, the organizer, Mavis Kerr, looked about her, and saw the Cheke Brass. Her stitchery cleverly suggests the texture and style of the Tudor costumes worn by the Chekes

5 Wedding kneeler for St John at Hampstead, designed by Barbara Thomson and worked by Dr Beryl Bolton.

6 Kneeler showing the coat of arms of the Turks and the Caicos Islands, from Christ Church, Woking, Surrey.

7 The bells of St Clement
Danes in the Strand,
designed by Nancy
Kimmins.

8 Design inspired by the
floor of the parish church
at Orta, in northern Italy,
by Barbara Thomson for
St John at Hampstead.

(husband and wife). (See also *Personal* and *Sacred and Secular*.)

The front and back pews in St Andrew, Hingham, Norfolk, have carved medallions of flowers and fruits. These appear impressively on kneelers with blue backgrounds and gold borders. The 12 angels carved upon the hammer beams of the roof, each carrying an Instrument of the Passion, are reproduced chiefly in *petit point*. (See also *Heraldry* and *Natural history*.)

A third of the kneelers in the Chapel Royal, Hampton Court Palace, East Molesey, Surrey, are based on the intricate pattern of the gold and blue Tudor ceiling. At St Mary, Byfleet, Surrey, they use as a link for their kneelers a design by Pat England taken from the quatrefoil on the font. There is nothing elaborate about the chessboard tiles on the floor of St Katharine, Knockholt, Kent, but they look well when embroidered. (See also *Stained glass*.)

If you go into the church of St Mary, Abbots Ann, not far from Andover in Hampshire, you can compare the kneeler designs with their origins in the window-glass. This may take a little while, but you will eventually discover the source of the attractively stylized flowers in the pews. Most unusual in origin are the virgin-crown kneelers, for here is the only church to perpetuate the medieval custom of awarding a crown on a virgin's death. By the west door details of the award are set out in an illuminated address; the crowns themselves hang in the roof until they disintegrate.

Mrs E. M. Scaramanga, whose husband, the Revd George A. Scaramanga, was rector at the time of the project, explains in her booklet on the Abbots Ann embroidery that each of these virgin-crown kneelers commemorates, with name and date, a woman of the parish who was awarded a crown.

We remember that, during the churchyard scene of *Hamlet* (*V.i.*), Ophelia's funeral is conducted with what Hamlet, standing apart, unseen, calls 'maimèd rites'; Laertes, Ophelia's brother, twice asks angrily 'What ceremony else?', whereupon the churlish priest says that Ophelia's death was 'doubtful', and that only a royal order has allowed her to have

> her virgin crants,
Her maiden strewments, and the bringing home
Of bell and burial.

'Crants' refers to the garland, or chaplet, worn as a sign of maidenhood, carried upon the bier, and later hung up in church.

Modern churches

Because they tend to be bare, lacking in colour and detail, modern churches are enriched by kneelers. They are often the first things people look at when entering.

At St Augustine of Canterbury, Kings Heath, Northamptonshire, each seat has its kneeler. Worked in trammed *gros point*, the original designs embody Christian symbols, chiefly in gold, cream and white on blue backgrounds. Sometimes a number of symbols – chalice, dove, fish, anchor, and so on – appear on a single kneeler. Yet, in designs so carefully considered, there is no hint of crowding. The sides, four inches deep, are also embroidered. A kneeler 33 feet long encircles the sanctuary. (See also *Wedding kneelers*.)

At All Saints, Spring Park, Croydon, built in 1956, Vera Sheppard tried to 'create our own history' by using the crests of church organizations and of local schools and colleges. The plain interior of St Richard, Ham, Surrey, is enlivened by pale green kneelers which tell the story of the patron saint in a sentence accompanied by a simple picture. Other contrasting designs are there – the Crucifixion, a pony cropping on a gold background – all fitting in with the pine roof and walls of this hexagonal church built in 1966.

Inside Guildford Cathedral the prevailing colour is pale beige – that is, until you look at the kneelers, 1,460 of them. All are different except for a diagonal dividing line that represents the slope from the town to Stag Hill where the Cathedral stands. Thus, half of the background is blue, half beige. This vast scheme began as far back as 1936 when Lady Maufe, wife of the architect, Sir Edward Maufe, founded the Cathedral Broderers' Guild and developed the idea for the kneelers which are, in effect, a history of the last 50 years. Every trade, every organization, that helped to create the building is recognized. The sheer scope of the enterprise has to be exciting; no wonder that, in one picture, scissors and needles honour the art of embroidery.

At St George, Oakdale, Poole, Dorset, a 25-year-old building, they decided to make identical kneelers with a central cross in red and green on a bold background in the body of the church, and a cross in gold and red on a blue background in the Mothers' Union Chapel.

The Church of the Good Shepherd, Haywards Heath, West Sussex, built in 1965, has been described as 'a Swiss chalet'. Its hundred kneelers have a basic design containing a Cross and a Good Shepherd on either side of a variety of central panels. The background Cross and Shepherd are all in the same colours, while the panels change.

So to a vicar's point of view. The Revd J. Michael Thompson, of The Ascension, Harrowby, in the parish of Grantham, Lincolnshire, confesses that in his small modern church, which has no stained glass, the embroidered kneelers fill a gap in symbolism. 'It is so handy,' he says, 'to have visual aids of this kind.'

St John, Corringham, Essex, a modern dual-purpose building (architect, Laurence King; opened in 1958) contains kneelers on biblical and hymn themes, with olive green as the basic colour. The altar kneelers, designed by Moreen Organ and worked by a group of half-a-dozen in cross stitch, form a panorama of the area. Another modern church, St Mary, Tattenham Corner and Burgh Heath, Surrey, is being equipped with 200 kneelers worked in several different stitches and designs (including lettering and Christian symbols), with grey-green backgrounds.

Finally, in Florida, the church of St Simon-on-the-Sound at Fort Walton Beach is 'fairly modern in tone with a light finish on the woodwork', according to Patricia Thornber. 'It has exposed beams and windows on the east which open on an enclosed garden; through windows on the west, the Sound can be seen.' Here the kneeler tops have shades of blue as a background; the sides are dark green with gold crosses to match the church carpet. Crested white waves and touches of red and purple on the shells add a few more colours. (See also *Christian symbols*.)

Natural history

Gardeners rush to eradicate lawn weeds as soon as they dare to appear. At Steep, near Petersfield in Hampshire, the vicar, Canon Douglas Snelgar, decided to commemorate them on the kneelers in All Saints Church, and so sprigs of dandelion and daisy are at the centre of two of the 150 kneelers he designed. As none is alike, the variety is astonishing and yet there is a

symmetry about the project as a whole. The emphasis is on design, not on pictorial effect. The arrangement of, say, oak leaves and acorns, or sprays of holly or mistletoe, seems made for the purpose. Four bullfinches fly with their wingtips touching and beaks facing inwards; spotted toadstools form a pattern; bats, butterflies, blackberries, appleblossom, ferns, rabbits, hedgehogs, trout, primroses – all these, and many more, stand out on dark or light blue backgrounds framed with a thin yellow border. A splendid game bird graces one kneeler. 'It doesn't really belong to Steep, but when it fell into the vicarage garden, although it soon flew away, I felt it should be included,' Canon Snelgar explained. He has been at Steep for 28 years, so he knows the flora and fauna brought to the village as the seasons come and go.

With help originally from the kneeler makers of Ickleton, Cambridgeshire, the Steep scheme began in 1967, lapsing temporarily when the organizer, Anne Winsum, could no longer see well enough to continue. In a village of 900 inhabitants they discovered lots of talent; among them, one old lady of 90 who had never done any needlework before. Once they got going, they could not stop. Using double canvas with ten threads to the inch, and working in cross stitch or long leg cross stitch, they needed innumerable shades of Appletons' crewel wool, and were left with suitcases full of small quantities. They kept to two tones of the same blue for backgrounds in the body of the church, and gold for those in the chapel. In all, a well-rounded scheme.

Upon the altar kneelers at All Saints, Ockham, Surrey, Mary Hanney gives to Downside Chapel, Hatchford Church (which is now demolished), and All Saints itself, their seasonal surroundings. So in the spring 'picture', a squirrel and a stoat come out into the sun, violets and daffodils are in bloom 'and the trees in leaf; on the winter kneeler a brace of pheasants stand alert on the snowy grass. To Ockham's basic motif of seven lancet windows, which links the kneelers in the body of the church, Mary Hanney has added her own country design: birds – among them a budgerigar – in flight above the churchyard or seen in its branches. This is an enchanting series organized by Joan Bowdon, assisted by Joan Brunton, Jane Black, Hanni and Ann Bailey, Elisabeth Holland, and Anthea Broughton. (See also *The church mouse*, *Heraldry*, *Stained glass*, and *Wedding kneelers*.)

High on a hill just north of the Cirencester–

67 Winter in Ockham: part of the altar rail kneeler designed and made by Mary Hanney for All Saints, Ockham.

68 Part of the altar rail kneeler at All Saints, Ockham. Designed and made by Mary Hanney.

Stroud road in Gloucestershire, in the little church of St Kenelm, Sapperton, birds, flowers, insects, and animals are delicately set in pale green backgrounds with darker borders. A former member of the choir left a request that money given in her memory should be spent on equipping kneelers for the choir stalls. On these and on kneelers in the pews – all worked in tent stitch on single canvas – ladybirds, butterflies, wasps, stoats, weasels, a snail, a fox, a grey squirrel on a tree, a pair of robins on a post, a donkey, a snowdrop, a buttercup, a daisy, a poppy, a sycamore leaf, all seem to belong to the *Cider with Rosie* country outside. For the altar kneelers the organizer, Lady Campbell, has worked a shell design in red and pink.

There are few buildings remaining in London which, outside Westminster, its Abbey and the great hammer-beamed Hall erected in the reign of Richard II, are there for us to see in the main as the men of the Middle Ages saw them. St Bartholomew the Great is one of these.

So said Ivor Brown. Here, among the Norman arches and Perpendicular clerestory, there are kneelers with blue backgrounds to match blue carpets. There is not much natural history left in this part of London, but in the Lady Chapel we find flowers all over the sanctuary kneeler, which is 24 feet long, 17 inches wide. A plaque explains that it was designed by Denise Williams who, with other members of the congregation and some overseas visitors, worked on it. The 600 City of London Squadron of the Royal Auxiliary Air Force, whose memorial is in the chapel, paid for the materials. It is made up of 1,036,800 stitches. (We wonder who counted them.)

The first Cornish church to produce a complete kneeler series was the fifteenth-century St Constantine in the village of that name, above a creek of Helford River. The two long altar kneelers in the Lady Chapel depict the wild flowers of Cornwall; they were worked by Paddy Mossop, wife of Canon R. O. Mossop, the vicar of Constantine 1950–73, and by Anne Westlake.

69   Seagulls, on a kneeler designed and made by Mrs R. Moore for All Saints, Brightlingsea.

70   (*Below left*) Fish, worked in Smyrna, tent, gobelin, and Parisian stitch, for St Lawrence, Eyam, Derbyshire.

Each took about three years to complete.

We have discovered that people like embroidering flowers more than anything else. Why, we do not know, but whatever the reason, there are many beautiful examples.

When you go under the carved Norman tympana and into St Swithin, Quenington, in the Cotswolds, you find yourself in an enchanted world of birds, animals and flowers. The heart of each kneeler is surrounded by bands of triangles in alternating dark and light blue, and a narrow border in yellow or pink. The effect is of a love of all creatures great and small; a bird chases a frog; an owl peers into the moonlit sky; a branch of fuchsia from the designer's garden looks real enough to pick.

The Quenington series has influenced others. Cynthia Hoyle told us: 'At St Stephen, Lansdown, Bath, we make no claim to remarkable skill or artistry, but for this it is only necessary to go about 40 miles to Quenington, whose village church is entirely furnished with beautiful kneelers.' Freda Holmes, of Udimore, Sussex, says that she went to Quenington and came back inspired. Presently she got friends to join her in making some for St Mary, Udimore. This was the first church in the neighbourhood to embroider kneelers; now nearly every other church has done so.

Aptly, for this orchard country, kneelers in Pershore Abbey, Worcestershire, are decorated with local fruits and vegetables. At All Saints, Croxley Green, near Rickmansworth, Hertfordshire, the theme is 'The Green'. All kneelers – including two worked by the vicar, the Revd Malcolm King – are embroidered with the flowers that grow there.

In the plain stone church of St Finnbarr, Dornoch, just above Dornoch Firth, a small congregation – 20 is regarded as a good attendance – is slowly but happily making kneelers. It is a familiar story. In 1983, when they decided that the church needed new kneelers, they ordered kits and these were duly completed; but because the kits were expensive, garish, and could be seen elsewhere, no one liked them much. Biddy Sandford then made an altar kneeler to her own design, an oyster-catcher on

the shore, which aroused interest, and several people announced that they would like to try something like it.

With Biddy Sandford as organizer, they composed a few simple rules. The design in the top panel must have 'something to do with the Highlands'. All designs must be the embroiderer's own work – that is, no transfers, and no duplicates, though copying picture postcards was allowed. The panel must be one of three different shapes: oval, diamond or rectangular. They used ten-stitches-to-the-inch canvas; cross stitch is worked over one strand, and the frame in which the design is placed consists of two rows of cross stitch in a suitable colour. The rest of the top, sides and ends are in cross stitch over two strands of canvas, using one or more of a choice of six shades of Wilton carpet wool. The junction of the top and sides is in long leg cross stitch to match the frame of the panel and to give a sharp edge. The corners are treated in the same way.

Subjects selected so far include roe deer, shelduck, ptarmigan, grey seals, violets, primroses, red grouse, wild cat, capercailzies, hedgehog, snow bunting, owl, rowan tree, heather, Highland cattle, salmon, Highland terriers, poppies and corn, and otter. If a traveller arrived at Dornoch late one Saturday night and attended kirk the next morning before setting out to explore the area, he would get a pretty good idea of what to expect from the kneelers in the pews.

The story ends as such stories usually end. In Biddy Sandford's words: 'It has been a matter of great satisfaction to me that 99 per cent of the people who vowed they could never design anything have managed to do so most successfully with a little help.'

At St Andrew, Bramfield, Halesworth, Suffolk, they chose to embroider wild flowers which, at first, were designed by a local artist. When he moved away, the vicar, the Revd John Murrell, took over. Only the tops were worked; they were then placed on wooden frames and the sides covered in green plastic. Among the flower studies at St John the Baptist, Findon, in Sussex, there are cornflowers, roses, tulips, arum lilies, and butterflies alighting on daisies. (See also *Local history* and *Wedding kneelers*.)

They have flowers and birds among their kneelers at St Andrew, Hingham, Norfolk; the flowers are placed inside a six-inch-square frame worked in gold. The series devoted to Norfolk birds, with gold and blue borders to match the

71   Stylized flowers for St Lawrence, Eyam, Derbyshire, worked in cross stitch and tent stitch.

72   Dog roses on a kneeler for Stratford St Mary, Suffolk.

altar carpet, furnishes the pews in which the Sunday School children sit. (See also *Funding*, *Hands across the sea*, *Heraldry*, and *Look about you*.)

Brightly coloured Hawaiian flowers will cover the altar kneelers at St Michael and All Angels, Lihue, Kanai. These, designed by a Hawaiian artist, Chris Faye, are worked in basketweave on 12 mesh canvas: a project, not yet completed, begun on her retirement by Barbara Scharla-Nielsen 'in lieu of tithing'.

Situated in an agricultural area, the church of St James, St Mary's, Ontario, has birds and flowers scattered along the 17-foot altar kneeler. The first of its kind in this part of Canada, it was created by Gwen Perkins, who sought the help of the Embroiderers' Guild.

The delicate flower studies at St James's, Hudson Heights, Jopijo, Quebec, are in *petit point*. The artist, Vi Eden Bryan, tells us: 'As this is a country church, designs from our wild flowers seemed more suitable than liturgical symbols.' Against olive green, the flowers include trilliums (worked by herself) and Dutchman's breeches (worked by the retiring vicar). 'Jack-in-the-Pulpit would have been more suitable for him, but even more difficult to do – I didn't think of it in time,' says Mrs Bryan.

At St David, Llanfaes, Brecon, Powys, they are making kneelers for the Lady Chapel with 12 different wild flowers as the main feature. They were chosen because, in Welsh, they are called after the Virgin Mary. Thus, marigold is Gold Mair; cowslip, Briallu Mair; snowdrop, Tapr Mair; St John's Wort, Ysgol Mair. Audrey M. Hargest planned these kneelers, which are worked mainly in tent stitch with some cross stitch. Each flower is placed on an oval panel with a contrasting background; the rest of the kneeler is blue. The altar kneeler has six panels, each containing two of the flowers.

Each of the altar-step kneelers in the sanctuary of St Peter's Anglican Church, Brockville, Ontario, is decorated with two biblical flowers and two biblical trees; there are also flowers and trees that grow in this part of Canada, by the St Lawrence River: columbine, violet, daisy, iris, buttercup, rose, trillium, moccasin flower; date, fig, cabob, olive, thorn, almond, pomegranate, mulberry. The litany kneeler has other 'natural' designs: star, mountains, water, whale, butterfly, chipmunk, lyre, horn, sun, moon, arrowhead, plum, bunchberry, wintergreen. (See also *Heraldry* and *Local history*.)

O all ye works of the Lord

Kneeler designs at the Collegiate Church of the Holy Trinity, by the river at Stratford-upon-Avon, have nothing to do with Shakespeare. This surprises some people; it may even annoy others. After all, they may say, Stratford is his birthplace; he did die there, and he is buried in the chancel. The debate will probably continue. The great thing is that these are lovely kneelers, the scheme has unity, and it is precisely planned. William Hawkes, a local architect and formerly churchwarden at Holy Trinity, admits that his idea for a design was accepted only after much discussion – though ultimately with enthusiasm. The *Benedicite* was to be the basis for the new kneelers. In one sense, he did consider the surroundings. For the background he chose 'a neutral but warm stone colour'. This is, in fact, the colour of the great pillars in this spacious cruciform building of air and light.

The decision to replace the kneelers came in 1975. The question asked was whether to have a single design or several. They had to overcome the familiar problem of varying levels of skill in embroidery, but if they had a single pattern this might cause interest to wane. To get over these two problems they decided finally to have a number of designs, and, to accommodate the less experienced needlewomen, a simple one which would be repeated for every third row. To avoid confusion between the two kinds of kneeler we will call them 'Design' and 'Text'.

The *Benedicite* suits this scheme of things superbly. By 'judicious juggling' (as William Hawkes describes the process), 'the verses could be adjusted to fit the church'. Thus, there are two rows of decorative kneelers ('Design') interspersed with a row of 'Text', which is, alternately, 'O all ye works of the Lord', and 'Praise Him and magnify Him for ever'. Altogether, 364 kneelers are required. Nearing completion, the scheme is directed by Mary Sykes. A total of 125 people have taken part, mostly from Stratford itself, and once a year they meet at Mrs Sykes's house.

So that the picture on the top of 'Design' kneelers and its name on the side can be seen together, they hang horizontally. Cross stitch is used throughout, in 69 colours of the French Laine Colbert DMC range. On 'Text' kneelers the sides and ends are worked in beige and brown in a pattern which has a Shakespearian association. It is derived from a Turkish rug in

73 The Benedicite, for Holy Trinity, Stratford-upon-Avon.

Hall's Croft, a splendid piece of Elizabethan domestic architecture in Old Town, Stratford, once the home of Shakespeare's elder daughter, Susanna, and her husband Dr John Hall, who were married at Holy Trinity in 1607. The Turkish rug pattern on the sides of 'Text' is replaced on 'Design' by a word or words to describe the subject and a pair of crosses potent.

The lettering on 'Text' is very beautiful; the lines are freely spaced and well balanced. The idea for it came from primitive Christian inscriptions. For 'Design', William Hawkes began by thinking of Romanesque mosaics, but as his confidence grew and the subject became harder, he 'ventured away from that style – not always wisely – for it seems clear that the more direct and simple the design, the more effective it usually is'.

That is for the visitor to Holy Trinity to judge. Certainly, the kneelers make an impression on many of the thousands who come into the church, especially in the summer. Tourists have been known to ask: 'Can we buy them?' William Hawkes is himself critical of some of the 'Designs' – the early ones, particularly. Of the very first, 'Angels of the Lord', he feels that the

colour range – red, orange, yellow – is undisciplined. 'We had not learned to keep changes of colour well marked,' he says.

Byzantine mosaics and a clear frosty night in March inspired 'Heavens', in which stars radiate from the earth, which contains a simplified map of Europe. For 'Waters that be above the firmament', he was again inspired by mosaics and also by watching streams in Wales flowing over stones.

When they reached the verse, 'O all ye powers of the Lord', it almost defeated them. Prolonged discussion with the clergy yielded only the unhelpful verdict that it should reflect 'God's essential life-giving force'. So, taking hints from science reference books, Mr Hawkes decided 'to show the DNA molecule with a pulsating background, as if a double helix had been unwound'. (We doubt if there is anything more deeply scientific on kneelers anywhere.) Next, from science to commerce. For 'Sun and moon' the Sun Alliance 'logo' provided a strong, clear design. 'Stars of Heaven' came from a mixture of Byzantine motifs and the *Star Wars* film. To produce a contrast with the stars in 'Heavens', these are more elaborate.

Presented with the problem of two kinds of dew, William Hawkes studied garden plants at dusk and dawn for 'O ye showers and dew', and for 'Dews and frost' he looked at hoar-frost on glass. 'Winds of God' was difficult; the solution, to have rolling spirals to suggest movement, developed from watching wind blowing leaves in circles.

Wood fires in winter gave him 'Fire and heat', and, for 'Winter and summer', the country at both times of the year was carried out in greens and browns. Unexpectedly, the idea for 'Frost and cold', in which bare branches stretch out, arose from a children's book, *The Winter Bear*, illustrated by Erik Blegvad. More obviously, for 'Ice and snow', photographs of Shackleton's and Scott's expeditions came to the rescue. This is suggested by blues, white and mauve, 'extraordinary colours that occur in ice and snow'.

Observation of the sky in the early morning gave the idea for 'Nights and days', in which the same earth as in 'Heavens' is accompanied by stars dying away at dawn. Close study of a candle flame in a dark room was the basis of 'Light and darkness', in which light, although surrounded by darkness, is strong enough to ensure that the darkness 'comprehendeth it not'. Taken from Victorian toy theatre sheets, lightning flashes dramatically against rain-laden clouds and forms the design for 'Lightnings and clouds'. A globe with Jerusalem picked out in gold appears on 'The Earth'. (A kneeler bearing this design has been presented to a Bombay church.)

For 'Mountains and hills' the designer copied Radnorshire hill scenery, and for 'Green things upon the Earth', an impression of a tropical rain forest grew from Douanier Rousseau's paintings; water forcing its way through hard rock as seen in illustrations of geological books is the 'Wells' design (though William Hawkes feels that the ASB translation, 'Springs', is better). 'Seas and floods' are powerfully suggested. Inspiration here: Hokusai's woodcuts of Mount Fuji. Dolphins and whales under water, while a wave pattern flows over them, is the design for 'Whales and all that move in the waters'. For 'Fowls of the air' there is an attempt to capture the feeling of flight; wild and primitive breeds, taken from books on cattle types and Thomas Bewick's wild bull, illustrate 'Beasts and cattle'; while for 'Children of men', TV shots that show commuters crossing London Bridge are intended to create a sense of distance. In 'Israel' the design aims to give the idea of selection by God. The hands reach upward as God makes His choice. (Derivation, of course, Michelangelo in the Sistine Chapel.)

The rest of the plan, still in draft, owes much to mosaics, William Blake, and books on the Old Testament world.

This is a highly original contribution to kneeler embroidery, and the fact that the designer acknowledges that some kneelers have not succeeded indicates a healthy approach. We wonder if he, Mary Sykes and members of her team have realized as they worked that the *Benedicite*, one of the loveliest of Canticles, is seldom chanted in these days when Matins is often omitted from regular Sunday services. You could say that the Stratford kneelers have rehabilitated 'ye works of the Lord'.

At another church, too, far away from Stratford, they drew their ideas for kneelers from the *Benedicite*. On 'needlepoint kneeling cushions' for the altar rail of the Church of the Good Shepherd, Norfolk, Virginia, 22 members of St Anne's Guild embroidered the opening words of the Song of Creation and symbols of 'All ye works of the Lord', from algae to the planets.

The sun and moon represent day and night; there are ears of wheat and bunches of grapes for Holy Communion. 'All ye fowls of the air', 'all that move in the waters', 'ye ice and snow', 'ye fire and heat' – all are present. For the seasons there are spring flowers and falling leaves; butterflies cross the canvas as symbols of eternal life. The apostles are presented as stars and also pictorially. St Matthew is a winged man with a book; St James the Less is given the club with which he was martyred, and St Bartholomew the flying knives which ended his life. Other symbols: St Andrew's cross, St John's poisoned chalice, St Peter's keys, St Simon's saw (instrument of his death), St Mark's winged lion, St Luke's winged ox.

The scheme was made possible by gifts of kneelers in memory of, or in honour of, friends or relations, and these were designed by Mili Holmes, an artist of New Canaan, Connecticut. Perhaps the St Anne's Guild needlepointers may one day visit Stratford-upon-Avon and compare their versions of the *Benedicite* with those at Holy Trinity.

The kneelers at the Church of the Good Samaritan, Villa Nova, Pennsylvania, form a sequence. Each kneeler, based on Genesis I, leads into the next. The first starts the quotation 'In the Beg–' and the second follows with '–inning'. On two others the words run on: 'Behold it/was very good.' The serpent's tail waves across one kneeler and its head appears on

74 The creation of the birds of the air, from the altar rail kneeler at St John's, Princes Street, Edinburgh.

76 The modern 'creation', showing an astronaut, a diver, and the Forth Road Bridge, from the altar rail kneeler at St John's, Princes Street, Edinburgh.

75 The creation of the heavens, from the altar rail kneeler at St John's, Princes Street, Edinburgh.

another; a flower is divided in half; a mountain range spreads over two kneelers. In this way a chain of 22 continuous pictures, designed by Gabrielle Haab, furnishes the 100-foot-long altar rail. The needlepointers drew lots for designs, and after just over five years the chain was complete. On Epiphany Sunday, 1985, they carried their kneelers in procession behind men in

costume as the Three Kings, who in turn carried gold, frankincense, and myrrh.

Altar kneelers at St John, Princes Street, Edinburgh, are unusual because they are worked on both top and bottom. During Lent they are turned over and the more austere design becomes visible. It is interesting to discover the different ways in which the Creation can be interpreted, as in painting. These artists take a wide view: God's creation of the world and His creatures are on the left with a chalice at the centre, and, on the right, modern creations: the atom bomb, astronauts, the Forth Road Bridge, actors, farmers, teachers. On the 'Lent' side a man and a woman (presumably Adam and Eve) kneel at each end on a ground cover of two blues (waves, perhaps). A crucifix stands at the centre.

To go round the chancel rail at St John, Woking, Surrey, embroiderers chose the Seven Days of Creation as their theme because it gave them scope for many individual versions. Kneelers were worked in a wide variety of stitches on single canvas, 14 threads to the inch.

For the 150th anniversary of St Michael, Highgate, north London, whose spire can be seen for many miles, Sylvia Green provided in 1982 new sanctuary kneelers of the Creation and the Fall. (See also *Wedding kneelers*.)

At Trinity Church, Princeton, New Jersey, they have 14 kneelers for the free-standing altar. The theme is Creation: 'They are joyful and beautiful', Carin Laughlin, who designed them, writes.

Peal of bells

For most people the name of the London church of St Clement Danes in the Strand must convey the sound of its bells, the jingle: 'Oranges and lemons/Say the bells of St Clement's.' Now here they are, swinging upon canvas for the sake of a kneeler.

The names of some Cornish saints ring like peals of bells. St Corentin, for example. Far down in the south of Cornwall this Celtic hermit founded the church dedicated to him at Cury. Later, Corentin became a Bishop in Brittany, which is why a recently uncovered mural in the nearby church of Breage shows him in cope and mitre. A Cury kneeler adds ringers' initials to a round of six bells. In St Mary-at-Latton, Harlow, Essex, one of the four bells on an altar kneeler is dated 1579. A pleasant design for the Diocesan Guild of Bellringers, at St Peter and St Paul, Deddington, Oxfordshire, consists of a golden bell with a red clapper and rope ends that demand to be pulled.

Personal

Among all the sacred symbols, wild flowers, birds and animals, crosses, ideas from stained glass windows and other architectural features, you will find some purely personal kneelers. This can happen only when there is freedom of choice. At St Mary the Virgin, Wimbledon, London, one worker reproduced her daughter's wedding bouquet; and Mary Loveband, organizer of the scheme, made a kneeler for a 90-year-old embroiderer who had done more than anyone else. It incorporates all her favourite things, including her dog. At St Nicholas, Thames Ditton, Surrey, a kneeler devoted to a map of the Falkland Islands was made by a woman whose son served in the 205 Signal Squadron there. At St John the Baptist in the Wilderness, Cragg Vale, near Hebden Bridge, Yorkshire, they are so proud of the fact that Jimmy Savile is an honorary churchwarden that his catchphrase, 'Jim'll Fix It', has now gone upon a kneeler.

In All Saints, Wickhambrook, Suffolk, built on Saxon foundations, it is surprising to find kneeler designs based on Maori art. This is because the Revd John Hodgson, who with his wife was responsible for them, was formerly a missionary in New Zealand. (See also *Antiques, Heraldry* and *Look about you.*)

Rich and rare

Not every kneeler is worked on canvas. Diana Springall, formerly chairman of the Embroiderers' Guild, designed a set of 12 for St Ann's Chapel in Lincoln Cathedral. Made of scarlet cowhide, they are inset with a circular set piece of canvas work in colours taken from the roundel windows above.

St Clement Danes, London, Wren's church in the Strand, has a curved east end; the necessarily curved altar kneeler is embroidered in crewel work in a flowing floral pattern.

For St John the Baptist, with its fifteenth-century tombs, by the river Windrush at Burford, Oxfordshire, Averil Colby evolved kneelers in patchwork. And at Middleham, Yorkshire, the altar kneeler, in the form of a knotted wool rug, bears the patronal names: St Mary and St Alkelda, 1280.

Buffalo skins cover kneelers in St Andrew's Presbyterian Church at Middlechurch, halfway between Winnipeg and Selkirk. Because it is within commuting distance of the city, the old rural character of the place is disappearing. The church also has buffalo skin seat covers, which were certainly welcome during winter in the old days when the only heating was by a large wood-burning stove. Boys (Lewis Nicholls reminds us) would be sent on early to get the stove going and to bring enough logs to see the service through. Usually a stove was placed in the middle of the church and the congregation sat as close to it as possible. (If you have ever experienced the chill of kneeling or sitting on wood in cold weather you will appreciate this.)

Most of the chancel kneelers at Christ's Church Cathedral, Hamilton, Ontario, are hooked. This technique, used principally for rugs, involves a hook (like a crochet hook), burlap, or hessian, and strips of fabric which are pulled through the backing to make a pile. Alice Robertson, of their Altar Guild, tells us that hooking has a long history in Canada. They went

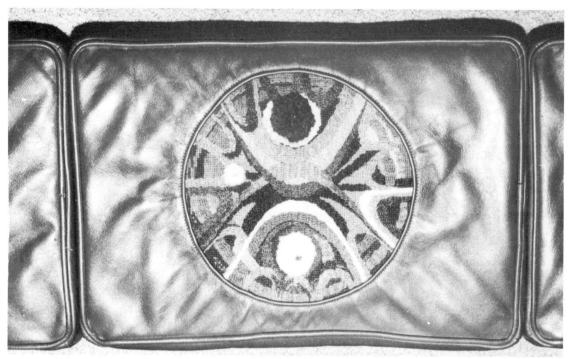

77   Scarlet cowhide, with a circular panel in tent, knot and velvet stitch, for Lincoln Cathedral. Designed by Diana Springall, past Chairman of the Embroiderers' Guild.

78   The arms of the Candlestick Makers' Guild, and a cushion for the Bishop's prie-dieu in Christ's Church Cathedral, Hamilton, Ontario. These are not embroidered, but 'hooked'.

79 General view of hooked kneelers for the canons' stalls in Christ's Church Cathedral, Hamilton, Ontario.

for inspiration to the symbolic altar rail carvings: slaughtered lamb, grapes on vine, lamb and flag and others. Designs for the Canons' stalls are crests of those who helped to build and decorate the Cathedral (for instance the Goldsmiths' Guild, and the Guild of Glaziers).

Sacred and secular

If a sociologist wished to collate the communal activities of the country, he could do no better than to look at kneelers (which are, in themselves, a communal activity). So many designers choose to depict local organizations, sacred and secular. Our research has yielded many examples: Sunday schools, Church of England Children's Society, missionary societies, Women's World Day of Prayer, Girls' Friendly Society, tennis clubs, Mothers' Union, Women's Institute, Girls' and Boys' Brigade, bowling clubs, under fives, the parish band, bellringers, campaigners, choirs, St John Ambu-

lance, youth clubs, British Legion, Royal National Lifeboat Institute, Missions to Seamen, conservation groups, Actors' Church Union, farmers' clubs, art groups. There must be several more.

Some groups have been content to reproduce badges, often from kits. At Bicton New Church, Shrewsbury, Shropshire, where many participants were elderly and had failing sight, they could do 'only the larger stitches and nothing too complicated', but, eager to provide extra kneelers to mark the church's centenary, they tackled Jacksons' designs for Guides, Brownies, Scouts, and other organizations.

Unusual ideas have emerged. At St Nicholas, Thames Ditton, Surrey, a handshake, cleaning materials, and a teapot and cup represent their Ladies' Care Guild; at St Andrew, Hingham, Norfolk, a dog training class is among many local bodies. At St Nicholas, Blakeney, Norfolk, the Guides' trefoil badge is adapted beautifully for the top of a kneeler, and matchstick figures in uniform stand on one side.

Stained glass

Many designers copy the stained glass colours in their church, though this is not always wise; much of it is pillar-box red and cobalt blue, and the result on kneelers can be harsh and unsubtle. Louisa Pesel would be horrified. There are exceptions, of course. At Mulbarton, Norfolk, kneeler colours complement those in the beautiful east window of St Mary Magdalene, and because windows in the nave are of clear glass, their colours do 'give a feeling of joy' (as Doreen Dean, responsible for the designs, describes it). Of 13 colours in nine designs, yellow, green, purple and blue predominate. Sets for each pew were worked in one of three shades to give the effect of light, medium and dark shafts of colour along the pews on both sides of the aisle. (See also *Local history* and *Words and music*.)

Stylized flowers occur on windows in the little Norman church of St Katharine, Knockholt, on the edge of the North Downs in Kent, and these have been transferred to the kneelers. Basically (in designs by Mrs N. O. Layton), the colours used are three shades of dull blue, red and gold, an effect restrained but satisfying. (See also *Look about you*.)

The seven rare lancet windows of All Saints,

Ockham, Surrey, link the kneelers there. On one, designed by Jane Black and worked by Elizabeth Holland, Dirck Pieters, a jolly Dutchman taken from the Flemish stained glass window, stands in front of the lancets. (See also *Natural history* and *Wedding kneelers*.)

Borders of windows designed by William Morris and Edward Burne-Jones in the Epiphany Chapel, Winchester Cathedral, suggested colours for kneelers there, and at St Mary, Fordingbridge, Hampshire, a design by Ruth Griffiths, taken from a stained glass madonna in one of the windows, has been worked on 75 kneelers in the main part of the church.

In the Victorian Gothic Church of St John, Woking, Surrey, they needed altar kneelers when the chancel was refurnished. At the Vicar's prompting they chose for their theme the Seven Days of Creation, worked to Janet Hazzard's designs in the colours of a stained glass window in the chancel. Mick Tapling was the organizer. (See also *O all ye works of the Lord*.)

Similarly, throughout the nave of St Anne's Episcopal Church, Abington, Pennsylvania, they have covered wooden kneelers with needlepoint tops, tracings of stained glass in the church. To 'bring the church colours to the altar', needlepointers at St Joseph, Boynton Beach, Florida, decided to join plans and colours – red, blue, green, turquoise and yellow – with

80 Dirck Pieters, a Dutch astronomer, copied from the Flemish stained glass window in All Saints, Ockham, Surrey. Designed by Jane Black.

81   The Arc de Triomphe and the tricolour of France, in Christ Church, Woking, Surrey.

82   The panda of China, in Christ Church, Woking.

83 The arms of the Turks and Caicos Islands, a dependency of the UK. This incorporates the Turks' head cactus, a queen conch shell, and a spiny lobster. In Christ Church, Woking, Surrey.

84 The thistle of Scotland, in Christ Church, Woking, Surrey.

those of the stained glass. Elsewhere, two altar kneelers designed and worked by Pauline Holin for the Good Samaritan Methodist Church, Addison, Illinois, are replicas, in blues, reds and yellows, of the window behind the altar. Other kneelers, completed recently for the Episcopal Parish Church of St Barnabas of the Valley, Cortez, Colorado, also use a set of stained glass patterns.

Designs taken from the windows are incorporated in kneelers for Lyttleton Street United Methodist Church, Camden, South Carolina. Merilyn Roll, who had long dreamed of the idea, mobilized a committee in 1984. After looking at various possibilities, visiting other churches, and getting in touch with artists, they settled finally on a group from North Carolina: a designer, a Scotch Wool Shop owner and an assistant.

Five stained glass windows, each for a continent, at the west end of Christ Church, Woking, Surrey, prompted the idea of kneelers which stand for various countries. Thus, they have the Arc de Triomphe with the tricolour of France; a panda for China; the flag of Sweden; the coat-of-arms of the Turks and Caicos Islands; and the thistle of Scotland. In addition, because of missionary associations, every kneeler bears on its front the Cross Crosslet. This variety of pattern could have been disastrous if it had not been so well conceived; but all the backgrounds are in the same gold colour, and only nine shades of wool were chosen, including black and white, though others could be added if a design required them.

In 1967 Gerald Bristow suggested that the old red hassocks should be replaced; a scheme

85   A simple alphabet.

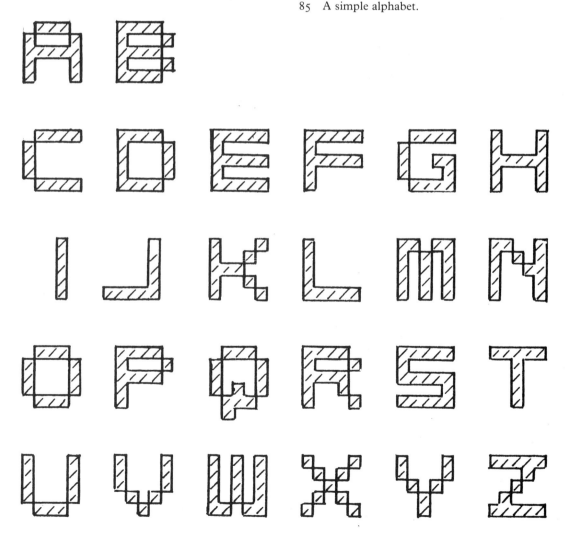

realized largely by himself, Lady Walker and Mrs Aplin – each of whom made over 20 kneelers – and by Elspeth and Jennifer Bristow, Mr and Mrs E. R. Amos, Vera Richmond, and the church architect, Mr A. E. Murray. The scheme was finished in February 1984.

These kneelers are hung on two hooks so that the top edge is a long one with the country's name in simple lettering. The short sides bear the initials of the worker and the date – again in simple standard letters that the architect approved.

Therapy

In one village the doctor tells patients suffering from depression that they would benefit from joining the kneeler group. At Thriplow, a small village near Royston, Cambridgeshire, a former churchgoer, aged 84 and now housebound, wanted to help with the project, so he was given a piece of canvas on which a simple cross had been painted. With his wife to thread the needles, he worked at his embroidery every morning. Almost rejuvenated in his enthusiasm, he made 13 kneelers, whereupon a neighbour aged 81 and his wife caught the infection, and both produced kneelers as well. Many people have praised the communal benefit of these schemes – and not exclusively among parishioners. As one organizer said: 'We brought together people who had not been actively connected with the church.'

At St Kieran, Campbeltown, Argyllshire, a woman approached Ursula Allen, the organizer, saying that she wished to make a kneeler 'as a Lenten penance'. She enjoyed this so much that she has been doing it ever since, and is their fastest worker. Here, too is the gratifying experience of kneeler makers at St Luke, Endon, near Stoke-on-Trent. Few had done any canvas work before, and at first they were hesitant; then hidden talents emerged. One of the most valuable things was the satisfaction beginners felt at their ability to cope; at the same time, many made new friends. More offers of help came from outside sources; people (teenagers among them) from a wide area joined, and by the time, seven years later, when the scheme (begun in 1968) was complete, 77 people had worked one or more kneelers, and seven others had contributed their special skills such as enlarging de-

signs and upholstering. Elizabeth Whitmore and Edna Bond were in charge.

'Most of all, the project united a group of very different individuals and created a group of friends.' This is how a needlepointer put it when a five-year project at the Church of the Good Samaritan, Villa Nova, Pennsylvania, finished. 'We wouldn't necessarily have become friends in any other way,' she said. 'Now, we don't want it to end. We plan to continue meeting once a month.'

'We had great satisfaction in doing all this embroidery and learning to perfect our skills.' Thus Mrs K. Barnes, of two projects: one of about 200 kneelers at Burlesdon, Hampshire, and the other at the extension church of St Paul on the local housing estate, where they made about 100. 'Though I left the parish in 1976,' she said, 'I have many happy memories of the kneeler classes, and the people met there.'

The 23 women who made the kneelers at St Peter, Brockville, Ontario, found (according to one member of the Altar Guild) that 'they loved it, hated it, would miss it, were glad to get it finished. However, they enjoyed working together, and developed friendships and a feeling of unity and purpose.'

Two by two

Some surprisingly different churches have made the choice of this kneeler subject: Noah's Ark. They include the National Cathedral in Washington, DC (foundation stone laid in 1907), which has a children's chapel with an altar kneeler decorated by Noah's Ark; and the little moorland church of St Edward, Shaugh Prior, South Devon, built between the mid-fourteenth and early sixteenth centuries, which also has Noah's Ark, complete with animals. The first three embroidered kneelers at Shaugh Prior were made in 1969 by a parishioner aged 88. In 1972, when they had new red carpets for the aisles, members decided that they should produce new kneelers, all with blue backgrounds and white-and-gold designs, and a small quantity of other colours where necessary. More animals, with St Francis, appear elsewhere.

With only a few embroiderers, it has taken a long time to complete just over 40 kneelers. Kathleen Searle, who is in charge, aims at a new one for each of the festivals – about three a year.

86 Tanker, designed by the tanker captain, who painted his ship on to squared paper, for All Saints, Brightlingsea.

They use double canvas, ten threads to the inch, and tapestry wool bought in hanks by the pound. (See also *In memoriam*.)

Noah's Ark goes very well in the series at All Saints, Brightlingsea, Essex, a fishing community. It is, after all, a kind of boat, one of many in the fleet represented here. (See also *Local history*.)

A rainbow appears above the Ark on an altar kneeler at Bethany United Methodist Church, Houston, Texas, and a dove carrying an olive branch approaches. (See also *Christian symbols*.)

Wedding kneelers

These are usually brought out only for the ceremony itself. Many are made from kits, but we have found some original examples as well. White or cream is a favourite colour for the background. Brides used to like a sprig of myrtle in their wedding bouquets, and in Kent a myrtle bush still blooms which came from a cutting of Queen Victoria's bouquet. One of the most charming arrangements is Hanni Bailey's for the wedding kneeler at All Saints, Ockham, Surrey, in which seven lancet windows form a background for two myrtle branches of creamy-white flowers and dark green leaves; bells and rings make up the rest of the design. (See also *The church mouse*, *Heraldry*, *Natural history*, and *Stained glass*.)

At St John the Baptist, Findon, Sussex, the bride's kneeler has a bouquet worked on a pale blue ground, and the bridegroom's has a Bible. All Saints, East Winch, Norfolk, contains a long wedding kneeler for both bride and groom, with a portrait of the church – restored in 1875 by Sir George Gilbert Scott – as the centrepiece, and wreaths of white flowers on either side. Diana Barrett, who designed this, completed it during 1985, having done several others at All Saints previously. (See also *Heraldry*.)

When Carol and Andrew Firth were married at St John the Baptist, Cragg Vale, near Hebden Bridge, Yorkshire, in August 1984, they were the first bridal pair to use two new wedding kneelers given by Carol's mother and grandmother. The old ones here were unpopular because they were uncomfortable to kneel on. (See also *Antiques* and *Personal*.)

Sylvia Green, in charge of embroidery at St Michael, Highgate, London, designed a bridal kneeler with a unicorn (for chastity), a crescent

87 Wedding kneeler designed by Hanni Bailey for All Saints, Ockham. The design includes myrtle, wedding bells, rings and a heart.

88 Wedding kneeler for St Michael's, Highgate, London. Designed by Sylvia Green and embroidered by Norah Edwards. The unicorn signifies chastity, the moon is a feminine symbol, and the small building represents the tabernacle of the body.

moon (for the glory of the Virgin Mother), and a small tabernacle (for the body). (See also *O all ye works of the Lord*.)

Every member of the congregation contributed some stitches to a wedding kneeler at St Augustine of Canterbury, Kings Heath, Northamptonshire; on each side this has a central cross and a wreath of white roses. (See also *Modern churches*.)

So, at length, to Canada where needlepointers at St Barnabas, St Lambert, Quebec, worked their all-white wedding kneelers in five different stitches.

Words and music

If in proportion and well spaced, lettering can look striking in canvas work. Many 'in memoriam' kneelers consist simply of names or initials and dates. In an old church, where rec-

89 Dedicated to Warwick Braithwaite, in Holy Sepulchre-without-Newgate. Worked in cushion, tent and rice stitch, and stem stitch.

ords are complete, the list of former incumbents can provide material for a series, as at Holy Trinity, Bosham, Sussex, and St Andrew, Hingham, Norfolk. At St Mary Magdalene, Mulbarton, also in Norfolk, on shaded backgrounds the words MARY and RABBONI (St John 20.16) again illustrate the art of lettering at its best. This is also true of the designs for trees, birds, and flowers at this church, which appear in simple capitals: ELM, ALDER, BIRCH; KESTREL, LARK, CUCKOO, OWL, PHEASANT; BLUEBELL, PRIMROSE, COWSLIP. (See also *Local history*.)

In many churches favourite texts emerge from plain backgrounds. At St John the Baptist, Puttenham, in Surrey, butterflies accompany 'All things bright and beautiful, All creatures great and small'; a font illustrates 'Suffer little children to come unto me', and a donkey assures us that 'The Lord hath need of me'. In a modern Surrey church, St Mary, Tattenham Corner and Burgh Heath, they have used words and phrases: 'Dominus'; 'Sanctus'; and 'Let everything that hath breath'. No more is needed. (See also *Disasters and triumphs*.)

The word PEACE in capitals appears on every kneeler in Wakefield Cathedral; and in the same

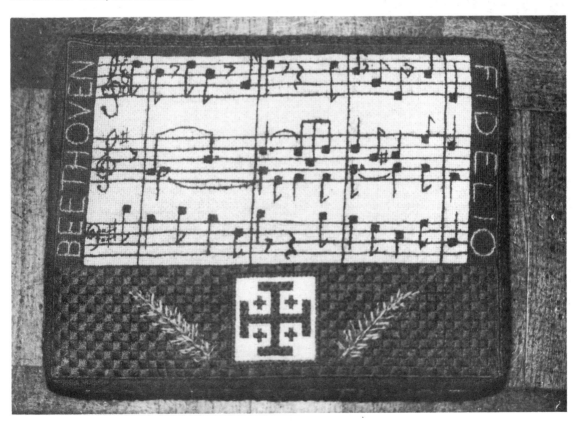

panel, behind Peace, embroiderers worked a word describing one of 12 industries or professions. Representing the ways people in the diocese make a living, they are Textiles, Local government, Mining, Baking and brewing, Engineering, Law and defence, Education, Chemicals, Distribution, Communication, Construction, and Medical. Because there are also 12 variations of colour schemes, only four of the 500 kneelers are identical.

Verses from the Psalms and the Beatitudes designed by Monika Stidham form the theme of kneelers at St Andrew's Episcopal Church, Amarillo, Texas. The Episcopal Churchwomen of St Andrew's began the project in 1976; it took several years to complete. 'We are very proud of them,' Anne Belville tells us.

90 Kneeler from Holy Sepulchre-without-Newgate in the City of London—the 'Musicians' Church', where all the musicians' kneelers are in blue with a Jerusalem cross in red on a white ground. Dedicated to F. Adrian Briggs, this one is worked in long leg, gobelin, Smyrna, and tent stitch.

In the Musicians' Memorial Chapel at Holy Sepulchre-without-Newgate, London (also known as St Sepulchre's), kneelers with bars of music – the Gloria in Excelsis Deo, a phrase from *Fidelio*, some Bach, Dvořák, Schubert, Brahms and Elgar – are perfect accompaniments to the stained glass windows for Sir Henry Wood and John Ireland. (See also *Hands across the sea*.)

The Lady Chapel of St Martin, Dorking, Surrey, is furnished with kneelers devoted to Ralph Vaughan Williams's music. Because his father, a priest in Gloucestershire, died when he was only two, he was brought up with his grandparents at Leith Hill Place, Dorking. In 1905 he founded the Leith Hill Music Festival – which still exists – and continued to run it until 1950. The kneelers, made in 1972, centenary of his birth, have bars of his music. Others that illustrate it include the overture and suite of *The Wasps*; the song sequence, *On Wenlock Edge*; the *Scott of the Antarctic* film; and *Rocket to the Moon*. There is one, too, with a picture of St

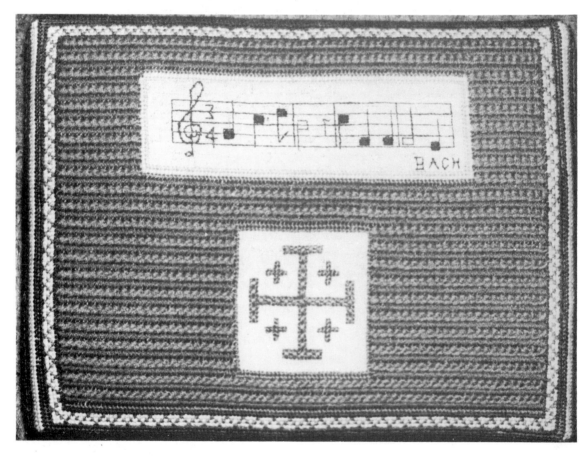

Paul's and Big Ben, for his London Symphony.

Another composer is recalled on a kneeler at St Mary, Barnes, London: Gustav Holst, who lived in Barnes. Charlotte Fuller has designed one in which a phrase of his music is enclosed beneath a church roof with (in the surrounding sky) the planets.

Embroiderers at the secluded Cotswold church of St Andrew, Sevenhampton, Gloucestershire, took as their inspiration Psalm 150, 'Praise ye the Lord', and worked a musical instrument on every choir kneeler. Thus, members of the choir may kneel now upon a pipe, a lute, a harp, a trumpet, or even 'the high-sounding cymbals'. (See also *Heraldry*.)

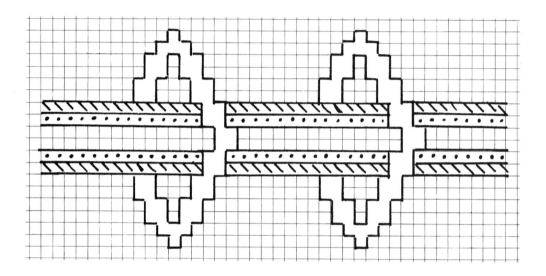

PART THREE

Churches with Embroidered Kneelers

England

Avon

Bath Abbey
Bath, All Saints, Carston
   „   , Royal School Chapel
   „   , St Mary the Virgin, Marshfield
   „   , St Stephen, Lansdown
Bathampton, St Nicholas
Bradford-on-Avon, Holy Trinity
Bristol, Christ the Servant, Stockwood
   „   , St Chad, Parkway
Burrington, Holy Trinity
Freshford, nr Bath, St Peter
Horton, St James the Elder
Kelston, St Nicholas
Westbury-on-Trym, nr Bristol, Holy Trinity
Weston-super-Mare, St John the Baptist

Bedfordshire

Bedford, St Peter de Merton with St Cuthbert
Clapham, nr Bedford, St Thomas of Canterbury
Dunstable, Priory Church of St Peter
Eaton Bray, St Mary
Flitwick, St Peter and St Paul
Leighton Buzzard, All Saints
   „   „   , St Barnabas, Linslade
Potton, St Mary
Upper Dean, All Hallows

Berkshire

Bucklebury, nr Reading, St Mary
Caversham, St Andrew
Cookham on Thames, Holy Trinity
Dedworth, nr Windsor, All Saints
Eton College Chapel
Hungerford, St Laurence
Newbury, St George, Wash Common
   „   , St Nicholas

Reading, All Saints
   „   , St Michael, Tilehurst
Shinfield, nr Reading, St Mary
Sonning, St Andrew
Stanford Dingley, St Denys
Sunningdale, Holy Trinity

Buckinghamshire

Aston-Sandford, St Michael and All Angels
Beaconsfield, St Mary and All Saints
Burnham, St Peter
Chalfont St Giles, St Giles
Chesham, Christ Church
Farnham Common, St John the Evangelist
High Wycombe, St Mary, Wooburn
   „   „   , St Paul, Wooburn
Marlow, St Peter
West Wycombe, St Laurence

Cambridgeshire

Cambridge, Girton College
Ely Cathedral
Great Shelford, St Mary the Virgin
Stapleford, St Andrew
Thriplow, nr Royston, St George
Waterbeach, St John the Evangelist

Cheshire

Bunbury, nr Tarporley, St Boniface
Heswall, St Peter
Little Moreton Hall, chapel
Nantwich, St Mary
Northwich, St John, Sandiway
   „   , St Luke, Winnington
Sandbach, St Mary
Stockport, St Martin, Norris Bank
Warrington, St Paul, Helsby
Weaverham, St Mary the Virgin

Cornwall

Constantine, nr Falmouth, St Constantine
Cury, St Corentin
Gunwalloe, St Winwaloe, Church Cove
Mawnan, nr Falmouth, St Maunanus
 and St Stephen
Penryn, nr Falmouth, St Gluvias
St Erth St Ercus,
St Uny, Lelant
St Neot, nr Liskeard, St Neot
Zennor, St Senara

Cumbria

Appleby, Almshouse Chapel
Carlisle, Holy Trinity, Wetherall
Crosthwaite, St Mary the Virgin
Walney Island, St Mary the Virgin
Workington, St Michael

Derbyshire

Chesterfield, St Peter and St Paul,
 Old Brampton
Derby Cathedral
Duffield, St Alkmund
Eyam, St Lawrence
Sudbury, All Saints
West Hallam, St Wilfred

Devon

Atherington, St Mary, High Bickington
Branscombe, St Winifred
Broadhempston, St John the Baptist, Woodland
Drewsteignton, nr Moretonhampstead,
 Holy Trinity
Exeter Cathedral
Exmouth, All Saints, Withycombe Raleigh
Great Torrington, St Michael
Hatherleigh, nr Okehampton, St John the
 Baptist
High Bickington, St Mary
Lapford, nr Crediton, St Thomas of Canterbury
Lydford, North Brentor Chapel, Christ Church
Ottery St Mary, St Mary
Pilton, St Mary the Virgin
Shaugh Prior, St Edward
Silverton, St Mary
Stoke-in-Teignhead, St Andrew
Stokenham, nr Kingsbridge, St Michael and All
 Angels
Tiverton, St Peter
Woodbury, St Swithin

Dorset

Affpuddle, St Lawrence
Blandford Forum, All Saints, Tarrant
 Keyneston
Blandford Forum, St Peter, Pimperne
Blandford St Mary, St Mary
Bridport, St Mary, Burton Bradstock
Compton Abbas, nr Shaftesbury, St Mary
Melbury Osmond, nr Dorchester, St Osmond
Poole, St George, Oakdale
Portisham, St Peter
Portland, All Saints
Sherborne Abbey, St Mary the Virgin
Wimborne Minster, St Cuthberga

County Durham

West Pelton, St Paul

Essex

Brightlingsea, All Saints
Chelmsford Cathedral
Chipping Ongar, St Martin
Colchester, St Leonard, Lexden
Corringham, St John the Evangelist
 „ , St Mary the Virgin
Dovercourt, All Saints
Harlow, St Mary-at-Latton
Henham, nr Bishop's Stortford, St Mary
Hornden-on-the-Hill, St Peter and St Paul
Ingatestone, All Saints, Stock
Kirby-le-Soken, nr Frinton, St Michael
Little Baddow, St Mary the Virgin
Shenfield, St Mary the Virgin
Thorpe-le-Soken, St Michael
Woodford Bridge, St Paul

Gloucestershire

Chipping Sodbury, St John the Baptist
Gloucester, St Michael, Brimpsfield
 „ , St Paul, Stroud Road
Icomb, nr Stow-on-the-Wold, St Mary
Longlevens, nr Gloucester, Holy Trinity
Newland, Cathedral of the Forest
Painswick, St Mary the Virgin
Quenington, nr Cirencester, St Swithin
Sapperton, nr Cirencester, St Kenelm
Sevenhampton, nr Cheltenham, St Andrew
Staunton, All Saints
Temple Guiting, St Mary the Virgin
Winchcombe, St Peter

Hampshire

Abbots Ann, St Mary
Awbridge, nr Romsey, All Saints
Boldre, nr Lymington, St John the Baptist
Burlesden, St Leonard
  ,, , St Paul
Catherington, All Saints
Compton, nr Winchester, All Saints
Crawley, St Mary
Crondall, All Saints
East Woodhay, St Martin
Ellingham, St Mary and All Saints
Farnborough, St Mark
Fleet, All Saints
Fordingbridge, St Mary
Froxfield, nr Petersfield, St Peter, High Cross
Hambledon, St Peter and St Paul
Hawkley, nr Liss, St Peter and St Paul
Houghton, All Saints
Lymington, St Thomas
Monk Sherborne, All Saints
Monxton, nr Andover, St Mary the Virgin
Porchester, Priory Church of St Mary
Portsmouth, St Nicholas
Ropley, nr Aslerford, St Peter
Silchester, St Mary the Virgin
Steep, All Saints
Stockbridge, St Peter
Sway, St Luke
Winchester Cathedral
Winchester, St Barnabas, Weeke
  ,, , St Lawrence

Herefordshire

Bodenham, St Michael and All Angels
Credenhill, St Mary
Hereford Cathedral
Hereford, Holy Trinity, Whitecross
  ,, , St Barnabas, Venn Lane
  ,, , St Mary, Callow
Pembridge, nr Leominster, St Mary
Ross-on-Wye, St Bridget, Bridstow
Tupsley, St Paul
Weobley, St Peter and St Paul

Hertfordshire

Borehamwood, All Saints
Elstree, St Nicholas
Gustard Wood, St Peter
Harpenden, St Nicholas
Hatfield, St Etheldreda
Much Hadham, St Andrew

Rickmansworth, All Saints, Croxley Green
  ,, , St Peter
Royston, All Saints
St Albans Abbey
St Albans, St Peter
St Paul's Walden, All Saints
Shillington, All Saints
Tring, St Peter and St Paul

Humberside

Alkborough, St John the Baptist
Cottingham, St Mary the Virgin
Kingston-upon-Hull, Holy Trinity
Snaith, nr Goole, St Lawrence

Kent

Appledore, St Peter and St Paul
Ashford, St Gregory and St Martin, Wye
  ,, , St Peter
  ,, , St Saviour
Bromley, St Andrew, Burnt Ash Lane
Canterbury Cathedral
Chatham, St Stephen and St Alban
Folkestone, St Eanswyth and St Mary
Harbledown, nr Canterbury, St Michael
Harrietsham, St John the Baptist
Horsmonden, St Margaret
Knockholt, St Katharine
Margate, St John-the-Baptist-in-Thanet
Newenden Church
Orpington, All Saints
Petts Wood, St Francis
Plaxtol, nr Sevenoaks (no dedication)
Rochester Cathedral
Ruckinge, nr Ashford, St Mary Magdalene
Sevenoaks, St John the Baptist
Teston, nr Maidstone, St Peter and St Paul
West Malling, St Mary
Whitstable, All Saints

Lancashire

Blackpool, Christ Church
Bolton, Christ Church, Harwood
Caton, St Paul
Colne, St Bartholomew
Croston, nr Chorley, St Michael
Heysham, St Peter
Kirkham, nr Preston, St Michael
Lancaster, Priory Church of St Mary
  ,, , St George in the Marsh

Leigh, St Peter
Leyland, nr Preston, St Andrew
Manchester Cathedral
Morecambe, Holy Trinity
Preston, All Saints
   ,, , St Cuthbert, Fulwood
St Anne's-on-Sea, St Anne
Salesbury, nr Blackburn, St Peter
Samlesbury, nr Preston, St Leonard-the-Less
Tunstall, St John the Baptist

Leicestershire

Fleckney, St Christopher
Knighton, St Guthlac, Holbrook Road
   ,, , St Mary Magdalene, Brinsmead Road
Melton Mowbray, St Mary, Ashby Folville
Woodhouse Eaves, St James-the-Great
   ,,   ,, , St Paul

Lincolnshire

Boston, St Botolph
Grantham, The Ascension, Harrowby
Kirton-in-Holland, nr Boston, St Peter and St Paul
Laceby, nr Grimsby, St Margaret
Lincoln Cathedral
Scotter, nr Gainsborough, St Peter
Scotton, nr Gainsborough, St Genewys
Spalding, St Mary and St Nicholas
Stamford, All Saints
   ,, , St John
Wainfleet, All Saints

London, City and Westminster

All Hallows-Berkyngechirche-by-the-Tower, EC3
Guy's Hospital, chapel
Holy Sepulchre-without-Newgate, EC1
Mary Sumner House, Tufton Street, SW1 (Mothers' Union), chapel
St Bartholomew the Great, Smithfield, EC1
St Clement Danes, Strand, WC2
St Mary-le-Strand, WC2
St Paul's Cathedral, EC2
St Thomas's Hospital, chapel, SE1
The Queen's Chapel of the Savoy, WC2
Westminster Abbey, SW1

Greater London

Barnes, St Mary, SW13
Chelsea Old Church, SW3
Chingford, St Peter and St Paul, E4
   ,, , Old Church, South Chingford, E4
Chiswick, St Nicholas, W4
Colindale, St Matthias, NW9
Crouch End, Christ Church, N8
Elgin Avenue, St Peter, W9
Eltham Park, St Luke, SE9
Finchley, St Mary-at-Finchley, N3
Fulham, St Etheldreda, SW6
Hampstead, St John-at-Hampstead, NW3
Highgate, St Anne, N6
   ,, , St Michael, N6
Royal Free Hospital, chapel, NW3
Southwark Cathedral, SE1
Wimbledon, King's College School, SW19
   ,, , St Mary, SW19

Merseyside

Liverpool Cathedral
Liverpool, All Hallows, Allerton
   ,, , St Hilda, Hunts Cross

Middlesex

Enfield, St Andrew
Gidea Park, St Michael
Harrow, St John the Baptist, Greenhill
Harrow Weald, All Saints
Hillingdon, St John the Baptist
Little Stanmore, St Lawrence
North Harrow, St Alban
Shepperton, St Nicholas
Sunbury-on-Thames, St Mary

Norfolk

Belaugh, nr Norwich, St Peter
Blakeney, St Nicholas
East Winch, All Saints
Great Yarmouth, St Mary Magdalene, Gorleston
Hingham, St Andrew
Holt, St Andrew
Hopton-on-Sea, St Margaret
Kenninghall, St Mary
Mulbarton, St Mary Magdalene
New Buckenham, St Martin
Norwich, St Faith, Horsham St Faith
   ,, , St Peter Mancroft
Salthouse, St Nicholas
Weston Longville, All Saints

Northamptonshire

Broughton, St Mary the Virgin
Crick, St Margaret
Earls Barton, All Saints
Fotheringhay, St Mary and All Saints
Northampton, All Saints, Harpole
  ,, , St Augustine of Canterbury, Kings Heath
Wellingborough, St Barnabas

Northumberland

Alnwick, St Mary, Lesbury
Hartburn, nr Morpeth, St Andrew
Heswall, St Peter
Holy Island (Lindisfarne), St Mary the Virgin
Newcastle-upon-Tyne, St Francis
North Shields, St George, Cullercoats

Nottinghamshire

Mansfield Woodhouse, St Edmund
Nottingham, Christ Church, Cinderhill
  ,, , St Mary Magdalene, Hucknall
West Bridgford, St Giles

Oxfordshire

Banbury, St John, Milton
  ,, , St Mary
Burford, St John the Baptist
Clanfield, St Stephen
Deddington, St Peter and St Paul
Didcot, All Saints, Chilton
Great Coxwell, St Giles
Hambledon, St Mary the Virgin
Islip, St Nicholas
Wootton, by Woodstock, St Mary
Yarnton, nr Oxford, St Bartholomew

Shropshire

Alberbury, St Michael and All Angels
All Stretton, St Michael
Bicton, Holy Trinity
Ellesmere, Blessed Virgin Mary
Halbarton, St Andrew
Onibury, St Michael
Portesbury, St George

Somerset

Ashill, Blessed Virgin Mary

Broadway, St Aldhelm and St Eadburga
Burnham-on-Sea, St Andrew
Curry Rivel, St Andrew
Donyatt, St Mary the Virgin
Glastonbury Abbey
Glastonbury, St John the Baptist
Horton, nr Ilminster, Parish Church
Ilchester, St Mary Major
Lacock Abbey
Long Sutton, St Michael, Somerton
Lyng, nr Taunton, St Bartholomew
Martock, All Saints
Minehead, St Michael, Nott Hill
North Cadbury, St Michael and All Angels
North Newton, nr Bridgwater, St Peter
Stoke St Gregory, St Gregory
Taunton, St Mary Magdalene
Thurloxton, nr Bridgwater, St Giles
Wells Cathedral

Staffordshire

Hanbury, nr Burton-on-Trent, St Werburgh
Maer, St Peter
Polesworth, Abbey Church of St Editha
Stafford, St Mary
Stoke-on-Trent, St Luke, Endon
Tunstall, St John the Baptist
Tutbury, St Mary
Whitmore, St Mary and All Saints

Suffolk

Aldeburgh, St Peter and St Paul
Assington, nr Bures, St Mary
Bardwell, St Peter and St Paul
Blundeston, St Mary the Virgin
Bury St Edmunds Cathedral
Chelmondiston, St Andrew
Corton, nr Lowestoft, St Bartholomew
Debenham, All Saints, Kenton
  ,, , St Mary Magdalene
Earl Stoneham, nr Stowmarket, St Mary
Flowton, nr Ipswich, St Mary
Framlingham, nr Woodbridge, St Michael
Great Bealings, St Mary
Halesworth, St Andrew, Bramfield
Ipswich, St Peter, Elmsett
Southwold, St Edmunds
Stanton, All Saints
Stratford St Mary, St Mary
Wickhambrook, nr Bury St Edmunds, All Saints
Westleton, St Peter

Surrey

Ashtead, St George
   ,, , St Giles
Badshot Lea, St George
Bramley, Holy Trinity
Brookwood, St Saviour
Byfleet, St Mary
Camberley, St Mary
   ,, , St Paul
Caterham, St Mary
   ,, , St Mary, Caterham on the Hill
Chiddingfold, St Mary the Virgin
Churt, St John the Evangelist
Cove, St John and St Christopher
Cranleigh, St Nicholas
Crondall, All Saints
Croydon, All Saints, Shirley
Dockenfield, nr Farnham, Church of the Good
  Shepherd
Dorking, St Martin
East Horsley, St Martin
East Molesey, St Paul
Effingham, St Lawrence
Elstead, St James
Epsom, St Martin
Epsom Downs, St Margaret, Great Tattenham
Esher, St George
Ewhurst, St Peter and St Paul
Fleet, All Saints
Great Bookham, St Nicholas
Guildford Cathedral
Guildford, All Saints
Ham, St Richard
Hampton Court Palace Chapel
Hascombe, St Peter
Hindhead, St Alban
Kew, St Anne
Lynchmere, St Peter
Merrow, St John the Evangelist
Newdigate, St Peter
Ockham, All Saints
Okewood, St John the Baptist
Ottershaw, Christ Church
Pirbright, St Michael
Purley, St Barnabas
Puttenham, St John the Baptist
Pyrford, St Nicholas
   ,, , Wisley (no dedication)
Redhill, St Matthew
Richmond, St Andrew, Ham Common
Ripley, St Mary the Virgin
Seale, St Lawrence
Shamley Green, Christ Church
Stoke d'Abernon, St Mary the Virgin

Tattenham Corner and Burgh Heath,
  St Margaret
Thames Ditton, St Nicholas
Wallington, Holy Trinity
Walton-on-the-Hill, St Peter
West Byfleet, St John the Baptist
Westcott, Holy Trinity
Weybridge, All Saints, New Haw
Windlesham, St John the Baptist
Woking, Christ Church
   ,, , St John
Wonersh, St John the Baptist

Sussex

Ardingly, nr Haywards Heath, St Peter
Bexhill-on-Sea, St Augustine, Cooden Drive
Bognor Regis, St Wilfred
Bosham, Holy Trinity
Brede, St George
Brighton, St Martin
   ,, , St Wulfran, Ovingdean
East Grinstead, St Swithin
East Wittering, St Anne
Eastbourne, St Michael and All Angels,
  Ocklynge
Goring-by-the-Sea, St Mary
Haywards Heath, All Saints, Lindfield
   ,, , Church of the Good Shepherd
Henfield, St Peter
Icklesham, St Nicholas and All Saints
Iford, St Nicholas
Kingston, St Pancras
Little Horsted, St Michael and All Angels
Newhaven, St Leonard, Denton
Poling, St Nicholas
Pulborough, St Mary Storrington
   ,, , St Mary, Thakeham
Rodmell, St Peter
Rye, St Mary the Virgin
Seaford, St Leonard
Stopham, St Mary the Virgin
Tangmere, St Andrew
Ticehurst, nr Wadhurst, St Mary
Uckfield, Holy Cross
Udimore, St Mary
Winchelsea, St Thomas the Martyr
Worthing, St Andrew, West Tarring
   ,, , St John the Baptist, Findon

West Midlands

Birmingham, Christ Church, Hagley Road West
   ,, , St Anne, Moseley

„ , St Faith and St Lawrence, Harborne
„ , St Francis
Coventry Cathedral
Coventry, St Barbara, Earlesdon
Leamington, All Saints
Long Compton, St Peter and St Paul
Stratford-upon-Avon, Holy Trinity
Sutton Coldfield, St John the Evangelist, Walmley
Whichford, St Michael

Wiltshire

Box, nr Corsham, St Thomas à Becket
Great Cheverell, St Peter
Lacock Abbey, St Cyriax
Lilbourne, St Peter, Milton
Mere, St Michael
Ramsbury, Holy Cross
Salisbury Cathedral
Tisbury, St John the Baptist

Worcestershire

Evesham, St Mary and St Milburgh, Offenham
Kington, nr Inkberrow, St James
Pershore Abbey

Yorkshire

Batley, St Paul, Hanging Heaton
Bedale, St Gregory
Beverley, St Mary
Bradford, St Peter, Allerton
Cragg Vale, nr Hebden Bridge, St John the Baptist in the Wilderness
Doncaster, St George
„ , St Nicholas, Thorne
„ , St Peter, Barnburgh
Eadale, nr Sheffield, The Holy and Undivided Trinity
Ellana, St Mary
Giggleswick, nr Settle, St Alkelda
Halifax, St Matthew, Lightcliffe
Haxby, St Mary
Kirk Hammerton, St John the Baptist
Lastingham, St Mary
Leeds, St Michael and All Angels, Headingley
Middleham, St Mary and St Alkelda
Nun Monkton, St Mary
Oxenhope, nr Keighley, St Mary the Virgin
Pickering, St Peter and St Paul
Ripon Cathedral
Rotherham, St Mary Magdalene, Whiston

Scarborough, St Martin-on-the-Hill
Sheffield, St John, Ranmoor
Wakefield Cathedral
York Minster

Scotland

Aberdeen, St John the Evangelist
Annan, Dumfries, St John (Episcopalian)
Campbeltown, St Kieran (Ep.)
Coldstream, St Mary and All Souls
Comrie, St Serf (Ep.)
Dollar, St James the Great (Ep.)
Dornoch, St Finbarr (Ep.)
Dunblane, St Mary (Ep.)
Dunfermline, Holy Trinity (Ep.)
Edinburgh, Christ Church, Falcon Road (Ep.)
„ , Holy Cross, Davidsons Mains (Ep.)
„ , St Fillan, Buckstone (Ep.)
„ , St John the Evangelist, Princes Street, (Ep.)
„ , St Mary's Cathedral (Ep.)
„ , St Michael and All Saints, Toll Cross (Ep.)
„ , St Peter, Lutton Place, Newington (Ep.)
„ , Western General Hospital Chapel
Falkirk, Christ Church (Ep.)
Falkland Palace, Fife, Chapel Royal
Forres, Moray, St John (Ep.)
Glasgow Cathedral (Church of Scotland)
Glasgow, St Gabriel, Govan (Ep.)
„ , St Mary's Cathedral (Ep.)
Haddington, Holy Trinity (Ep.)
Invergowrie, All Souls
Iona Abbey
Killin, St Fillan (Ep.)
Kirkcudbright, St Francis Greyfriars (Ep.)
Largs, St Columba (Ep.)
Lockerbie, All Saints (Ep.)
Portree, Isle of Skye, St Columba (Ep.)
St Andrews, All Saints (Ep.)
Wick, St John the Evangelist (Ep.)

Isle of Man

Ballaugh, St Mary
Bride, St Bridget
Port St Mary, St Mary
„ , St Peter

Wales

Amroth, Pembrokeshire, St Elidyr
Brecon, St David
Burry Port, St Mary
Gilwern, nr Abergavenny, St Elli
Llandaff Cathedral
Llandrindod Wells, Old Parish Church
    ,,   ,,   , Cefnllys
    ,,   ,,   , Holy Trinity
Llantwit Major, Glamorgan, St Donat
Newport, Monmouthshire, Cathedral Church of
    St Woolos
Oakwood Pontrhydyfen, Port Talbot, St John
Oystermouth, Swansea, Clyne Church
Pontblyddyn, nr Mold, Christ Church
St David's, St David's Cathedral
Swansea, Collegiate and Parish Church of
    St Mary

Ireland

Belfast, St Patrick, Newtownards Road
Dublin, St Patrick's Cathedral
Glengariff, Co. Cork, Holy Trinity
Groomsport, Co. Down, Parish Church
Kildare, Cathedral of St Brigid
Killaloe, Cathedral of St Flannan

France

Paris, the American Cathedral

Israel

Jerusalem, St George's Cathedral, Anglican

Portugal

Estoril, St Paul, Anglican

Zambia

Lusaka Cathedral

United States of America

Arizona

Clarkdale, St Thomas
Green Valley, St Francis-in-the-Valley
Paradise Valley, Christ Church of the Ascension
Scottsdale, St Barnabas in the Desert
Sedona, St Andrew
Sun City, St Christopher
Tucson, St Philip's in the Hills
Wickenburg, St Alban

Arkansas

Altheenier, United Methodist Church
Folville, St Peter's on the Prairie
Forrest City, First United Methodist Church
    ,,   ,,   , Good Shepherd Episcopal
Jonesboro, First United Methodist Church
Little Rock, Church of Christ, Episcopal
Magnolia, First United Methodist Church
Pine Bluff, First United Methodist Church
West Memphis, Holy Cross

California

Altadena, St Mark
Berkeley, St Mark
Beverly Hills, All Saints
Carmel, All Saints
Carmel Valley, St Dunstan
Coronado, St Dunstan
Del Mar, St Peter
Englewood, Holy Faith Church
Glendale, St Mark
Hanford, Church of the Savior
La Canada, St George
La Crescenta, St Luke's of the Mountains
Laguna, St Mary
Lajolla, St James-by-the-Sea
Long Beach, St Luke
Los Angeles, Cathedral Church of St Paul
    ,,   ,,   , Diocesan House
    ,,   ,,   , St Athanasius
    ,,   ,,   , St Barnabas
Orinda, St Stephen
Palas Verdes Estates, St Francis

Pasadena, All Saints
Poway, St Bartholomew
Riverside, St George's Mission Church
„ , All Saints
San Diego, All Saints
„ „ , Christ Church
„ „ , St Andrew's by the Sea
„ „ , St Luke
„ „ , St Paul
San Francisco, St Aidan
„ „ , St James
San Gabriel, Church of our Savior
San Merino, St Edmund
Santa Barbara, Trinity Church
South Pasadena, St James
Ventura, St Paul
Whittier, St Matthias

Colorado

Colorado Springs, Chapel of Our Savior
„ „ , United States Air Force
Academy
Cortez, Saint Barnabas of the Valley
Denver, Cathedral Church of St John-in-the-
Wilderness
Denver, Christ Church
„ , Church of the Ascension
„ , St Mark
„ , St Philip and St James
Fort Collins, St Luke
Fort Morgan, St Charles the Martyr
Golden, Ascension Church
Lakewood, St Paul
Littleton, St Timothy
Pueblo, Calvary Episcopal Church

Connecticut

Avon, Christ Church
Bridgewater, St Mark
Brookfield Center, St Paul
Essex, St John
Fairfield, St Paul
Greenwich, Christ Church
„ , St Barnabas
Hebron, St Peter
Middlebury, Christ Church
Middleton, Church of the Holy Trinity
Mystic, St Mary
New Canaan, St Mark
New London, St James
Newton, Trinity
Old Lyme, St Anne
Rocky Hill, St Andrew the Apostle

Southport, Trinity Church
Stonington, Calvary Church
West Hartford, St John

Delaware

Greenville, Christ Church Christiana Hundred
„ , St Peter
Highlands, Wilmington, Emmanuel Church
Lewes, Cathedral of St John
Wilmington, Christ Church of Christiana
Hundred

Florida

Boynton Beach, St Joseph
Cocoa, St Mark's Episcopal Church
Fort Walton Beach, St Simon-on-the-Sound
Jacksonville, Church of the Redeemer
Longwood, Christ Church
Orlando, Cathedral Church of St Luke
„ , St Michael
Sarasota, Church of the Redeemer
„ , St Mark
Winter Park, St Richard

Georgia

Athens, St Phillip
Clarksville, Grace Church
Macon, Christ Church
Savannah, Christ Church

Hawaii

Lihue, Kanai, St Michael and All Angels
Maui, The Chapel, Seabury Hall Girls' School

Illinois

Addison, Good Samaritan Methodist Church
Aurora, Trinity Church
„ , St David's Episcopal Mission
Batavia, Calvary Church
Chicago, Cathedral Church of St James
„ , Church of the Atonement
„ , St Chrysostom
Evanston, St Luke
„ , St Mark
„ , St Matthew
Flossmoor, St John
Geneva, St Mark
Glencoe, St Elizabeth
Glenellyn, St Mark
Highland Park, Trinity Church

Hinsdale, Grace Church
Jacksonville, St John's Cathedral
Kenilworth, Church of the Holy Comforter
La Grange, Emmanuel Church
Lake Forest, Church of the Holy Spirit
Lansing, Church of Christ the King
Mt Prospect, St John
Naperville, St John
Northbrook, St Giles
Oak Park, Grace Church
Park Ridge, St Mary
Rockford, Emmanuel Church
St Charles, St Charles' Church
Western Springs, All Souls
Wheaton, Trinity Church
Wilmette, St Augustine
Winnetka, Christ Church

Indiana

Angola, Holy Family
Indianapolis, Christ Church Cathedral
    ,,   , St Alban's
Logansport, Trinity
Marion, Gethsemane
Michigan, City, St Andrew's-by-the-Lake
    ,,   ,,   , Trinity Church
Richmond, St Paul
South Bend, Church of the Holy Trinity

Kansas

Topeka, Grace Cathedral
    ,,   , St David
Winfield, Grace Episcopal Church

Maine

Gardiner, Christ Church
Northeast Harbor, St Mary's-by-the-Sea
Winter Harbor, St Christopher's-by-the-sea

Maryland

Bethesda–Chevy Chase, St John
Chevy Chase, All Saints
Cumberland, Emmanuel Parish Church
Silver Spring, Grace Church

Massachusetts

Adams, St Mark
Beverley Farms, St John
Dedham, St Paul

Feeding Hills, St David
Hawickport, Christ Church
Holyoke, St Paul
Lenox, Trinity Church
Longmeadow, St Andrew
Natick, St Paul
Palmer, St Mary
Pittsfield, St Stephen
South Hadley, All Saints
Springfield, St Luke
West Springfield, Good Shepherd
Worcester, All Saints

Michigan

Alma, St John
Ann Arbor, St Clare of Assisi
Bloomfield Hills
Calumet, Christ Church
Cranbrook, Christ Church
Detroit, Christ Church
    ,,   , St Paul's Cathedral
    ,,   , St Timothy
Grand Rapids, Grace Church
    ,,   ,,   , St Mark
Grosse Point, Christ Church
    ,,   ,,   , Grosse Point Memorial Church
    (Presbyterian)
    ,,   ,,   , St Michael
Ironwood, Church of the Transfiguration
Lansing, St Paul
Saginaw, St John

Minnesota

Albert Lea, Christ Church
Wayzata, St Edward

Mississippi

Laurel, Ascension

Missouri

Fulton, Winston Churchill Memorial,
    Westminster College
Kansas City, Central United Methodist Church
    ,, ,, , Grace and Holy Trinity Cathedral
St Louis, Christ Church Cathedral
    ,, ,, , Church of the Holy Communion
    ,, ,, , St Matthew
    ,, ,, , St Michael and St George
    ,, ,, , St Peter

Montana

Billings, St Stephen

Nebraska

Kearney, St Luke

New Hampshire

Hopkinton, St Andrew
Keene, St James
Portsmouth, St John
Sugar Hill, St Matthew

New Jersey

Atlantic City, St James
Bernardsville, St Bernard's Parish
Beverly, St Stephen
East Orange, St Paul
Essex Fells, St Peter
Gladstone, St Luke
Ho-ho-kus, St Bartholomew
Jersey City, St Paul
Kinnelon, St David
Lebanon, Church of the Holy Spirit
Madison, Grace Church
Maplewood, St George
Merchantville, Grace Church
Middletown, Christ Church
Morristown, St Peter
Mount Holly, St Andrew
Princeton, All Saints
   ,, , Princeton Chapel
   ,, , Trinity Church
Riverton, Christ Church
Somer's Point, Christ Church
South Orange, Church of St Andrew and Holy
   Communion
Summit, Calvary Church
Upper Montclair, St James
Woodstown, St Luke

New Mexico

Carlsbad, Grace Episcopal Church

New York

Albany, Cathedral of All Saints
Bay Shore, LI, St Peter
Brooklyn, NYC, All Saints
Garden City, LI, Cathedral of the Incarnation

Geneva, Trinity Church
Hempstead, LI, St George
New York City, St James
   ,,   ,,   ,, , Trinity Church
Oyster Bay, LI, Christ Church
Pelham, Christ Church
Pittsford, Christ Church
Rochester, Saint Paul's
West Point, West Point Chapel

North Carolina

Asheville, All Souls
   ,, , Grace Memorial
   ,, , Trinity
Bat Cave, Transfiguration
Black Mountain, St James
Blowing Rock, St Mary's of the Hills
Brevard, St Phillip
Chapel Hill, Chapel of the Cross
Gastonia, St Mark
Greensboro, Holy Trinity
Hickory, Church of the Ascension
Lexington, Grace Church
Little Switzerland, Episcopal Church
Raleigh, Diocese of NC Headquarters Chapel
Shelby, Church of the Redeemer
Southern Pines, Chapel of the Terraces
Tryon, Church of the Holy Cross
West Asheville, St George

Ohio

Canton, United Methodist Church of the Savior
Cincinnati, Church of the Redeemer
   ,, , Grace Church
   ,, , Indian Hill Church
   ,, , St Paul's Chapel, Church House
Glendale, Christ Church
Middleton, Church of the Ascension

Oklahoma

Oklahoma City, St Paul's Cathedral
Tulsa, Trinity Church

Pennsylvania

Abington, St Anne
Ardmore, St Mary
Bethlehem, Trinity Church
Bryn Mawr, Church of the Redeemer
Chestnut Hill, All Saints Hospital
Gibsonia, St Thomas-in-the-Field

Langhorne, St James
Paoli, Church of the Good Shepherd
Philadelphia, St Paul
Pittsburgh, Trinity Cathedral
Swarthmore, Trinity Church
Villa Nova, Church of the Good Samaritan
Wyncote, All Hallows

Rhode Island

Greenwich, St Luke
Newport, Emmanuel Church

South Carolina

Bennettsville, St Paul
Camden, Lyttleton Street United Methodist
  Church
Charleston, Cathedral of St Luke and St Paul
Clemson, Holy Trinity
Columbia, St Mary
Florence, All Saints
Hilton Head Island, St Luke
Spartanburg, Church of the Advent
Summerville, St Paul
Sumter, Holy Comforter

Tennessee

Memphis, Calvary
  „   , Grace – St Luke
  „   , Holy Communion Church
  „   , St Elizabeth
  „   , St John
  „   , St Mary's Cathedral
Sewannee, Chapel of the University of the
  South

Texas

Alvin, Grace Church
Amarillo, St Andrew
  „   , St Peter
Baytown, Trinity
Dallas, St John
Freeport, St Paul
Georgetown, Grace Church
Houston, Bethany, United Methodist
  „   , Christ Church Cathedral
  „   , Church of the Holy Spirit
  „   , Church of the Redeemer
  „   , St Christopher
  „   , St George
  „   , St John the Divine

  „   , St Martin
  „   , St Peter the Divine
Lampasas, St Mary
Lubbock, St Paul's-on-the-Plains
Lufkin, St Cyprian
Marlin, St John
Odessa, St John
San Antonio, Cathedral of St John
Temple, Christ Church
Waco, St Paul

Vermont

Burlington, Cathedral Church of St Paul
Manchester Center, Zion Episcopal Church

Virginia

Charlottesville, Church of Our Savior
Ivy, St Paul
McLean, St John's Langley
  „   , St Thomas
Norfolk, Christ and St Luke
  „   , Church of the Good Shepherd
Portsmouth, Trinity Church
Roanoke, St John
Stanton, Faith Evangelical Lutheran
The Plains, Grace Church

Washington

Anaconter, Lutheran Church
Bellevue
Darrington, Church of the Transfiguration
Goldhap, Diocesan Camp Huston
Marysville, St Philip
Seattle, Church of the Epiphany
  „   , Church of the Good Shepherd
  „   , St Elizabeth
  „   , St John the Baptist
  „   , St Mark's Cathedral
  „   , St Thomas, Medina
  „   , Trinity Church

West Virginia

Beckley, St Stephen
Martinsburg, Trinity Church
Shepherdstown, Trinity Church
Wheeling, Laurencefield Chapel
  „   , St John
  „   , St Matthew

Wisconsin

Delavan, Christ Church
Eau Claire, Christ Church Cathedral
Fort Atkinson, St Peter
Lacrosse, Christ Church
Milwaukee, Christ Church
„ , St John

District of Columbia

Washington, Cathedral of St Peter and St Paul
(National Cathedral)
Washington, Little Sanctuary, St Alban's
School
Washington, St Dunstan
„ , St John, Lafayette Square
„ , St Margaret
„ , St Patrick's Episcopal Church
„ , Trinity Lutheran Church

Canada

Alberta

Calgary, Cathedral Church of the Redeemer,
Three Hills

British Columbia

Kelowna, St Michael and All Angels
Pouce Coupe, Christ Church, Anglican
Surrey, St Christopher, Saturna Island
Vancouver Island, Shawnigan Lake Boys'
School

Manitoba

Winnipeg, Christ Church

New Brunswick

Hampton, St Paul
St John East, All Saints

Nova Scotia

Halifax Cathedral
West Northfield, St Andrew's, Anglican

Ontario

Belleville, St Thomas
Brockville, St Peter's, Anglican, Pine Street
Burlington, St Luke
Fonthill, Holy Trinity
Hamilton, Christ's Church Cathedral
„ , Grace, Anglican
Kingston, Cathedral Church of St George
Lambeth, Trinity, Anglican
London, Church of the Transfiguration
„ , St Paul, Anglican
Maitland, St James, Anglican
Markham, Grace Church, Anglican
Milton, Grace Church
Niagara on the Lake, St Mark, Anglican
Oakville, St Jude
Peterborough, St John, Anglican
St Mary's, St James
Toronto, Bishop Strachan School
„ , Grace Church on the Hill
„ , Havergal College
„ , St George's United
Woodstock, St Paul's Anglican

Quebec

Hudson Heights, Jopijo, St James
Montreal, Christ Church Cathedral
„ , St Philip, Anglican, Montreal West
Ottawa, Christ Church Cathedral
St Lambert, St Barnabas
Tadoussac, Protestant Chapel (open July and
August only)

Saskatchewan

Saskatoon, St Timothy

Australia

Canberra, Australia Capital Territory

Aranda, Church of the Holy Covenant
Canberra, Boys' Grammar School Chapel
„ , St John
Deakin, St Luke
Ginalong, St Simon
O'Connor, St Philip
Reid, St John
Sutton, St Peter
Weston, St Peter

New South Wales

New South Wales

Albury, St Mark's North Albury
Artarmon, St Basil
Avalon, St Mark
Barraba, St Mark
Bellevue Hill, Cranbrook School Chapel
Bowral, St Jude
Burwood, St Paul's Anglican Church
Campbelltown, St Peter
Campsie, St John
Cobbitty, St Paul
Darling Point, St Mark
Gordon, St John's Anglican Church
Goulburn, Bishopthorpe Chapel
   „   , St Nicholas
   „   , St Saviour's Cathedral
Haberfield, St Oswald
Hornsby, Barker College Chapel
Hunter's Hill, All Saints
Killara, St Martin
Kurrajong, St Stephen
Lane Cove, St Andrew
Lindfield, St Auburn
Mildura, Anglican Church
North Sydney, St Thomas
Pejar, nr Goulburn, St Stephen
St Ives, Christchurch
Sydney, St Andrew's Cathedral
Turramurra, St James
Wahroonga, Abbotsleigh School for Girls
   „   , St Andrew
Watson's Bay, HMAS Watson Chapel
West Lindfield, All Saints
Windsor, St Mathew
Young, St John the Evangelist

Northern Territory

Alice Springs, Anglican Church

Queensland

Brisbane, Lutheran Church
Toowoomba, St James
   „   , St Luke

South Australia

Adelaide, Chapel of St Augustine, Pulteney
   Grammar School
Adelaide, St Peter's College Chapel, Hackney
   „   , St Theodore, Rose Park
   „   , St Theodore, Toorak Gardens
   „   , Walford House Chapel, Girls Grammar

School, Hyde Park
Bordertown, Church of England
Campbelltown, St Martin
Crafers, Church of the Epiphany
Elizabeth Downs, St Catherine
Glenelg, St Peter
Seacliff, All Saints
Somerton, St Phillip

Victoria

Alexandra, St John's Anglican Church
Ballarat, Ballarat Grammar School Chapel
Camberwell, St John
   „   , St Mark
Caulfield, St Mary
Corio, Geelong Grammar School Chapel of All
   Saints
East Malvern, St John's Anglican Church
East Ringwood, Holy Trinity
Frankston, St Luke
Hawthorn, St Columb
Mansfield, Geelong Grammar School at
   Timbertop
Melbourne, St Patrick's Cathedral
   „   , St Paul's Cathedral
   „   , St Peter Eastern Hill
   „   , Trinity College Chapel, Melbourne
University
Mildura, St Margaret
Mt Eliza, Peninsula Boys' School Chapel
Ormond, Church of Christ
South Yarra, Melbourne Grammar School
   Chapel of St Peter
South Yarra, Christ Church
Swan Hill, Christ Church

New Zealand

Ashburton, St Stephen
Auckland, Bishopsdale Chapel
   „   , King's College Secondary School Chapel
King's College Preparatory School Chapel
King's College, Diocesan School for Girls
   Chapel
Barhill, Anglican Church
Dunedin, Dunedin Hospital Chapel
   „   , Wakani Hospital Chapel
Hamilton, St Luke, Melville
   „   , St Peter's Cathedral
Invercargill, Chapel of the Southland Hospital,
   Kew

Morrinsville, St Matthew
Nelson, Christ Church Cathedral
„   , Stoke Church
New Plymouth, Taranaki Base Hospital, Chapel
  of the Good Shepherd
Remuera, King's School Chapel
Wellington, Cathedral of St Paul

This list is inevitably incomplete, and we shall be glad to hear of any additions. Readers should write to the authors c/o B.T. Batsford, 4 Fitzhardinge Street, London WIH OAH

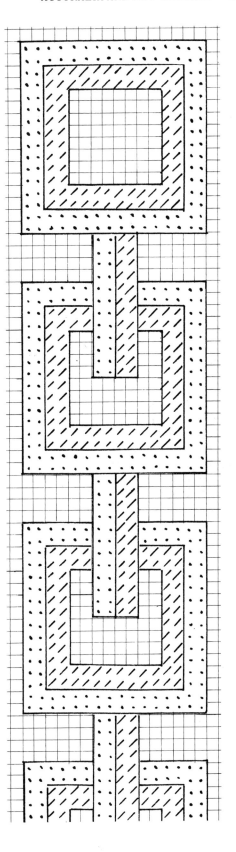

Some books and pamphlets

Cynthia Brown, *Hassocks For Your Church: How We Made Them at Great Bealings*

Dorothy Carbonell and Hugh Carey, *Embroideries of Winchester Cathedral*, 1975

Catalogue of the 'Kneelers from Churches in the Guildford Diocese' Exhibition, 1984

Chelmsford Cathedral, guidebook by Geoffrey Wrayford, 1984

Church Kneelers, J. & P. Coats, Book No. 1058

Church Needlework 2: Canvas Work, Embroiderers' Guild

Church of the Good Shepherd, Norfolk, Virginia: St Anne's Guild Pamphlet, 1980

Beryl Dean, *Ecclesiastical Embroidery*, Batsford, 1958

A Directory of Ecclesiastical Embroidery, National Association of Diocesan Altar Guilds of the Episcopal Church of the USA, 1979

Joan Edwards (compiler), *A Picture Book for Kneeler Makers*, Bayford Books, 1984

Embroidery Designs in St Patrick's Chapel, Glastonbury Abbey, Somerset, Glastonbury Abbey Trust Publications No. 3, 1979

Fifty Canvas Embroidery Stitches, J. & P. Coats, Book No. 1218

Ida and David Fraser Harris, *St Constantine in Cornwall: A Brief Guide*

Jennifer Gray, *Canvas Work*, Batsford, 1974, 1985

In His House: The Story of the Needlepoint Kneelers, Christ Church Cathedral, Montreal, Canada

Lucy Judd, *Embroideries in Salisbury Cathedral*

Kneeler Project, 1980, Wakefield Cathedral

Winifred Lockwood, *Exeter Cathedral Tapestry*, 1985

Mary P. Olsen, of South Brookville, Maine, USA, *For the Greater Glory*

W. Ellwood Post, *Saints, Signs and Symbols*, SPCK, 2nd edition 1981

Mary Rhodes, *Dictionary of Canvas Work Stitches*, Batsford, 1980

Saint Botolph's Church, Boston (Lincolnshire), *Kneelers*

Saint Mary-at-Latton Church, Harlow (Essex), *A Short History*

E. M. Scaramanga, *The Embroideries of Abbots Ann Church*

The Treasures of Time: Embroidered Kneelers in Chelsea Old Church

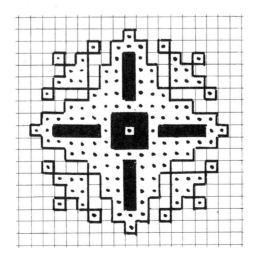

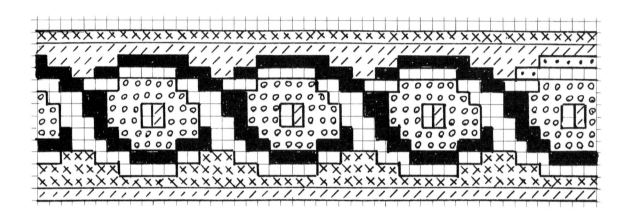

Suppliers

United Kingdom

De Denne Ltd
159–161 Kenton Road
Kenton
Harrow
Middlesex HA3 0EU

The Embroidery Shop
51 William Street
Edinburgh EH3 7LW

Foamplan Ltd
164 Holloway Road
London N7 8DD
Reconstituted foam FP5

Latex Cushion Company
  (Birmingham) Ltd
Ecclesiastical Division
830 Kingsbury Road
Erdington B
Birmingham B24 9PU
*This firm can supply fillings,
and will make up kneelers*

Hugh Mackay & Co. Ltd
PO Box 1
Durham
Can provide thrums, but please contact in advance

Needle Needs
20 Beauchamp Place
London SW3 1NQ

The Royal School of Needlework
25 Princes Gate
London SW7

The Weavers' Shop
Carpet Factory
Barford Road
Bloxham
Oxfordshire

Woodward Grosvenor & Co. Ltd
Stourvale Mills
Green Street
Kidderminster
Worcs DY10 1AT
Can provide thrums, but please contact in advance

USA

The Dotted Needle
805 N. Rosser
Forrest City
Arkansas 72335

Fiddlesticks
620 Coral Street
Honolulu
Hawaii 96813

Canada

The Silver Thimble Inc.
64 Rebecca Street
Oakville
Ontario
Canada L6J 1J2

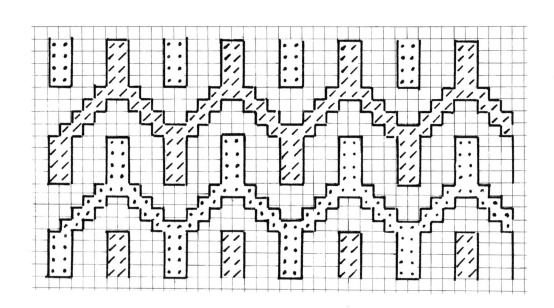

Index